THE PORSCHE 911 BOOK

NEW REVISED EDITION

PHOTOGRAPHS BY RENÉ STAUD

TEXTS BY JÜRGEN LEWANDOWSKI

teNeues

INTRODUCTION

JÜRGEN LEWANDOWSKI

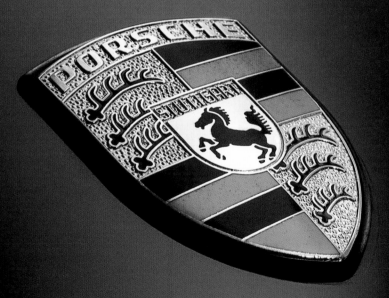

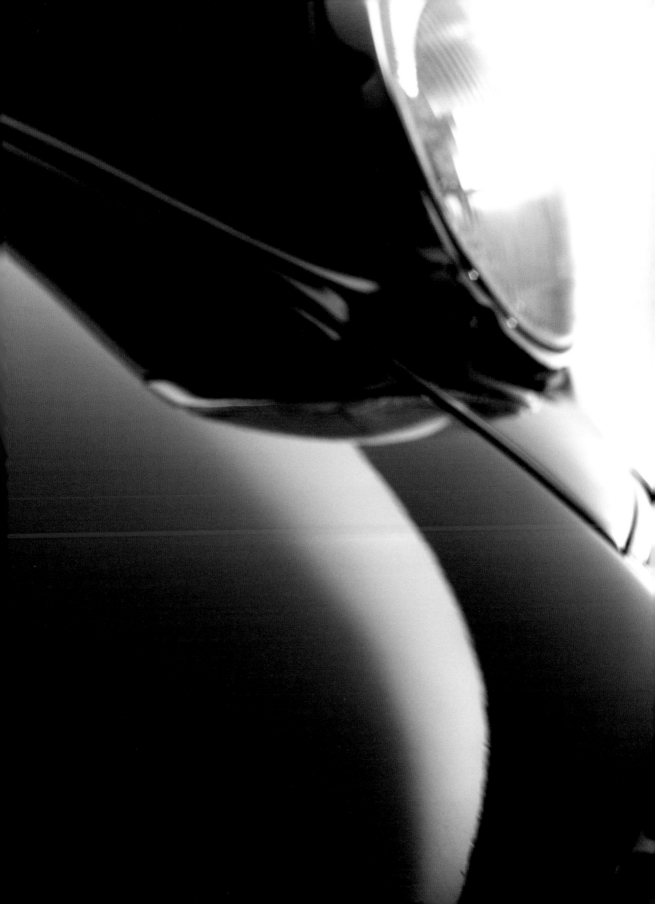

911: Supposedly a random sequence of numbers—in automotive reality the code word for the most successful sports car in the history of the automobile, the victor in thousands of races and a legend that for more than half a century has reinvented itself time and again, yet without losing sight of its roots.

Naturally things were going well for the still-young Porsche Company in the 1950s: sales of the 356 were considerably stronger than Ferry Porsche could ever have dreamt. At the unveiling in spring of 1948, Ferry Porsche had hoped to sell at least the planned 50 vehicles relatively easily; when the 356 series was discontinued in 1965, he could look back on an impressive 77,766 specimens built. By the mid-1950s, it was clear to all at Porsche that a successor model would need to be ready some day—and yet the genesis of the new Porsche became more difficult, more labored than it would appear today.

And even that Thursday, September 12, 1963, the day of its world premiere, the 901—the model was not dubbed the "911" until the vehicles were delivered to their new customers—was still not completely developed. That is why the 356 had to mutate into the 356 C with a few model facelifts, remaining in production until 1965, so that enough money could be earned to complete Project 901. No, the 901/911 was no easy task, and it swept the then-young firm to the brink of bankruptcy.

As it turned out, though—thanks to the brilliant contours designed by Ferdinand Alexander "Butzi" Porsche, and thanks to the wonderful 2-liter, six-cylinder boxer engine—the model had tremendous promise. At a glance, one could see it was a timeless beauty, and the hoarse sound of the air-cooled, six-cylinder engine promised performance, adventure and racing success. Those with an interest were content to wait patiently until November 1964, when the first vehicles were delivered. It also helped that the first customers casually overlooked the vehicle's weaknesses and had no difficulties helping perfect the car as paying test drivers.

Looking back on the world premieres at the Frankfurt Motor Show in 1963, one discovers lots of cars that have since been forgotten. Some became legends but went out of production decades ago. But more than 50 years later, the 911 is still alive, and it seems to grow younger from one series to the next. Whatever demands were made of it, they were fulfilled: turbocharger, winning series, targa roof, convertible, speedster, four-wheel drive, double-clutch transmission—it was all feasible, and still is. It mastered all of the safety and environmental legislation with flying colors, won thousands of races and seems to be immortal. Ferry Porsche once said: "The last car ever built will be a sports car." He was too modest and too clever to have said: "The last car ever built will be a Porsche 911." But that probably would have been the truth.

911: Eine vermeintlich zufällige Aneinanderreihung von Ziffern – in der automobilen Realität das Codewort für den erfolgreichsten Sportwagen der Autogeschichte, den Sieger in Tausenden von Rennen und eine Legende, die sich seit über einem halben Jahrhundert immer wieder neu erfindet, ohne ihre Wurzeln zu vergessen.

Natürlich ging es der noch jungen Firma Porsche in den 1950er Jahren gut: Der 356 verkaufte sich wesentlich besser, als sich das Ferry Porsche jemals erträumt hätte – während er bei der Vorstellung im Frühjahr 1948 noch gehofft hatte, wenigstens die geplanten 50 Fahrzeuge einigermaßen gut verkaufen zu können, blickte er, als die 356-Baureihe dann 1965 eingestellt wurde, auf beeindruckende 77 766 gebaute Exemplare zurück. Dennoch war man sich bei Porsche bereits Mitte der 1950er Jahre darüber im Klaren, dass eines Tages ein Nachfolger parat zu stehen hatte – jedoch: Die Genese des neuen Porsche geriet schwieriger und mühsamer, als es heute den Anschein erweckt.

Und selbst am Donnerstag, dem 12. September 1963, dem Tag seiner Weltpremiere, war der 901 – die Bezeichnung 911 sollte der Porsche erst bei der Auslieferung der Kundenfahrzeuge erhalten – noch nicht fertig entwickelt, weshalb auch der 356 mit einigen Modellpflegemaßnahmen noch zum 356 C mutieren und bis 1965 weiter gebaut werden musste, damit Geld für die Fertigstellung des Projekts 901 verdient werden konnte. Nein, der 901/911 war keine leichte Geburt und er brachte die noch junge Firma an den Rande des Bankrotts.

Doch er entpuppte sich – dank der genialen Form von Ferdinand Alexander „Butzi" Porsche und des wunderbaren 2-Liter-Sechszylinder-Boxermotors – als großartiges Versprechen.

Man sah ihm auf Anhieb seine zeitlose Schönheit an und der heisere Klang des luftgekühlten Sechszylinders versprach Leistung, Abenteuer, Rennerfolge. So warteten die Interessenten geduldig bis zum November 1964 als die ersten Fahrzeuge ausgeliefert wurden – und dass die ersten Käufer über die Schwächen des Fahrzeugs locker hinwegsahen und keine Probleme damit hatten, als zahlende Versuchsfahrer zu der Perfektionierung des Fahrzeugs beizutragen, half auch.

Wer heute einen Blick auf die Weltpremieren der Frankfurter Automobil-Ausstellung 1963 wirft, wird viele Autos entdecken, die vergessen sind. Manche wurden zu Legenden, doch ihre Produktion wurde bereits vor Jahrzehnten eingestellt – der 911 ist jedoch seit über 50 Jahren am Leben und es scheint, dass er von Baureihe zu Baureihe jünger wird. Welche Wünsche auch immer an ihn gestellt wurden, er hat sie erfüllt: Turbolader, Seriensieger, Targa-Dach, Cabriolet, Speedster, Allradantrieb, Doppelkupplungsgetriebe – alles war und ist machbar. Er meisterte alle Sicherheits- und Umweltgesetze mit Bravour, gewann Tausende von Rennen und scheint unsterblich. Ferry Porsche sagte einmal: „Das letzte Auto, das gebaut werden wird, ist ein Sportwagen." Er war zu bescheiden und zu klug, um zu sagen: „Das letzte Auto, das gebaut werden wird, ist ein Porsche 911." Aber das wäre wohl die Wahrheit gewesen.

911 : une suite de chiffres apparemment laissée au hasard ; dans le monde de l'automobile, le code derrière lequel se cache le plus grand succès en matière de voitures de sport de l'histoire automobile, une voiture qui a remporté des milliers de courses et une légende qui ne cesse depuis plus de cinquante ans de se renouveler, sans oublier ses racines.

Naturellement, la société Porsche, encore jeune, se portait bien dans les années 50 : les ventes de 356 dépassaient largement tout ce dont Ferry Porsche avait jamais rêvé : lors de son lancement au printemps 1948, Ferry Porsche espérait au moins vendre à peu près facilement les 50 véhicules programmés. Lorsque la série 356 fut définitivement stoppée en 1965, le nombre d'exemplaires vendus atteignait le chiffre impressionnant de 77 766. Cependant, chez Porsche, on savait dès le milieu des années 50 qu'il faudrait prévoir un jour un successeur.

Même le jeudi 12 septembre 1963, le jour de sa première mondiale, la 901 – la Porsche ne devait hériter de sa désignation 911 que lors de la livraison des véhicules clients – n'était pas encore finalisée, c'est pourquoi le modèle 356 fut enrichit de quelques évolutions et se transforma en 356 C pour continuer d'être commercialisé jusqu'en 1965 afin de gagner suffisamment d'argent pour faire aboutir le projet 901. Ah ça non, l'avènement de la 901/911 n'a pas été un accouchement facile ! Et il a même poussé la jeune entre-prise au bord de la faillite.

Pourtant le modèle se révèle vite extrêmement promet-teur grâce à la forme géniale inventée par Ferdinand Alexander « Butzi » Porsche et le magnifique moteur boxer six cylindres de 2 litres. On reconnut tout de suite en elle une beauté intemporelle, tandis que le grondement rauque du six cylindres à refroidissement à l'air était comme une promesse de performance,

d'aventure, de succès en course. Les prospects attendirent ainsi jusqu'en novembre 1964 pour la livraison des premiers modèles. Le fait que les premiers acheteurs fermèrent complaisamment les yeux sur les faiblesses du véhicule et ne trouvèrent rien à redire à jouer le rôle de conducteur d'essai payant pour contribuer au perfectionnement du véhicule a bien aidé l'entreprise.

Si, aujourd'hui, vous jetez un regard en arrière sur les premières mondiales de l'exposition automobile de Francfort en 1963, vous découvrirez de nombreuses voitures que l'on a depuis oubliées. Certaines sont devenues des légendes, mais leur production s'est arrêtée il y a plusieurs décennies déjà ; tandis que la 911, elle, mène son existence depuis plus de cinquante ans et semble rajeunir de série en série. Quels que soient les souhaits que l'on a pu formuler à son égard, elle les a tous comblés : turbocompresseur, vainqueur en série, toit Targa, cabriolet, speedster, traction à quatre roues motrices, boîte de vitesses à double embrayage, tout est possible, hier comme aujourd'hui. Elle a vaincu avec bravoure toutes les lois relatives à la sécurité et à la protection de l'environnement, a remporté des milliers de courses et semble immortelle. Ferry Porsche a dit un jour : « la dernière voiture qui sera construite sera une voiture de sport. » Il était trop modeste et trop intelligent pour dire : « la dernière voiture qui sera construite sera une Porsche 911. » Pourtant cela aurait été la vérité.

A LEGEND IS BORN

1959–1963

A LEGEND IS BORN

In the mid-1950s, the professionals at Porsche began thinking about a successor to the 356. It was clear that in the long term the four-cylinder engine in the 356 would not be able to grow beyond a 2-liter engine capacity and 130 hp in everyday driving—while on the other hand the desire for a roomier interior and luggage compartment was heard more often. People began organizing their thoughts on the subject in 1957, and by 1959 the prototype had been built: the green T7 that later evolved into the 901, a model designed by Ferdinand Alexander Porsche and unveiled in a world premiere on September 12, 1963, at the IAA in Frankfurt. By mid-1964, exactly 82 specimens had been built of this near-series pilot model, a model that was never offered for sale. Series production began on September 14, 1964—under the model name that remains to this day: 911.

DIE GEBURT DER LEGENDE

Mitte der 1950er Jahre begann man sich bei Porsche Gedanken über einen Nachfolger für den 356 zu machen, denn es wurde klar, dass der Vierzylinder des 356 langfristig nicht über 2 Liter Hubraum und 130 alltagstaugliche PS wachsen konnte – andererseits wurde immer öfter der Wunsch nach mehr Innen- und Kofferraum geäußert. 1957 begann man, die Ideen zu ordnen und 1959 entstand als Prototyp der grüne T7, aus dem dann der von Ferdinand Alexander Porsche gestaltete 901 wurde, der am 12. September 1963 auf der IAA in Frankfurt Weltpremiere feierte. Von diesem seriennahen Vorserienmodell, das nie in den Verkauf kam, entstanden bis Mitte 1964 exakt 82 Exemplare, bevor am 14. September 1964 die Serienproduktion begann – nun mit der bis heute gültigen Bezeichnung 911.

LA NAISSANCE D'UNE LÉGENDE

Chez Porsche, au milieu des années 50, on commença à penser à un successeur pour le modèle 356, car il était clair que le quatre cylindres de la 356 ne pourrait pas, à long terme, dépasser les 2 litres de cylindrée et les 130 CH au quotidien. D'autre part, la demande de plus d'espace dans l'habitacle et dans le coffre se faisait de plus en plus fréquente. En 1957, on commença à rassembler et mettre en ordre les idées et en 1959, le prototype vert T7 vit le jour, puis devint par la suite le modèle 901, dessiné par Ferdinand Alexander Porsche, qui fêta sa première mondiale le 12 septembre 1963 au salon IAA de Francfort. Ce modèle de pré-série proche de la série, qui ne fut jamais commercialisé, a été construit en exactement 82 exemplaires jusqu'au milieu de l'année 1964, avant que ne démarre la production en série, le 14 septembre 1964, avec la désignation qu'on lui connaît aujourd'hui encore, la 911.

Year of manufacture	1959
Engine capacity	2,195 cc
Power	120 hp / 88 kW
Transmission	four-speed transmission
Weight	1080 kg / 2,380 lbs.
Acceleration	not measured
Top speed	not measured
Quantity produced	1 model

Year of manufacture	1963–1964
Engine capacity	1,991 cc
Power	130 hp / 96 kW
Transmission	five-speed transmission
Weight	1080 kg / 2,380 lbs.
Acceleration	0–100 km/h in 9.1 seconds
Top speed	approx. 210 km/h / 130 mph
Quantity produced	82 pilot models

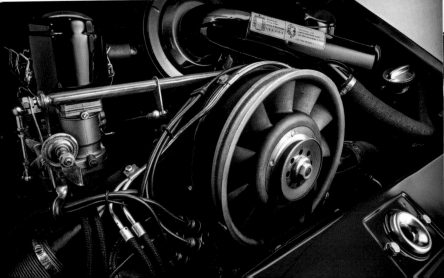

THE 911 SAGA BEGINS

1963–1973

THE 911 SAGA BEGINS

A year after the world premiere in Frankfurt, the time had come: the first, long-awaited 911 models were delivered, with 130 hp of power and a top speed of 130 mph—and by December 31, 1964, another 235 specimens had been delivered to their new owners. At a base price of DM 21,900, though, the 911 was considerably more expensive than the 356 SC that had been available for DM 16,500 until 1965. So in 1965, the 912 was added to the program that linked the contours of the new coupé with the 90-hp four-cylinder engine of the 356. Priced at DM 16,250, it served as an entry-level model. And with calls for a convertible 911 growing louder all the time, 1966 witnessed the issue of the first Targa, with a stowaway plastic rear window that was replaced by fixed glass in the 1969 model year. Then, in 1969, the engine capacity rose to 2.2 liters, and beginning in 1971 a 2.4-liter engine with up to 190 hp in the S version provided speeds of nearly 145 mph. Thanks to limited-edition models such as the 911 R, the 911 S 2.4 TdF or the 911 S 2.5, the 911 was successful in racing sports right from the start, helping fuel the myth of the brand with hundreds of victories in rallies and circuit races.

DER BEGINN DER 911-SAGA

Ein Jahr nach der Weltpremiere in Frankfurt war es so weit: Die ersten lange erwarteten 911 wurden ausgeliefert, nun mit 130 PS Leistung und einer Höchstgeschwindigkeit von 210 km/h – und bis zum 31. Dezember 1964 konnten noch 235 Exemplare ausgeliefert werden. Doch der 911 war mit einem Basispreis von 21 900 Mark deutlich teurer als der bis 1965 für 16 500 Mark angebotene 356 SC – deshalb kam 1965 der 912 ins Programm, der die Form des neuen Coupés mit dem 90 PS starken Vierzylinder-Motor des 356 verband und für 16 250 Mark als Einstiegsmodell fungierte. Und da der Ruf nach einem offenen Elfer immer lauter wurde, erschien 1966 auch der erste Targa, noch mit einer herunterklappbaren Kunststoff-Heckscheibe, die im Modelljahr 1969 durch eine feste Glasscheibe ersetzt wurde. 1969 stieg dann der Hubraum auf 2,2 Liter, und von 1971 an sorgten 2,4 Liter Hubraum und bis zu 190 PS in der S-Variante für 230 km/h. Dass der 911 auch von Anfang an im Rennsport erfolgreich agierte, war limitierten Modellen wie dem 911 R, dem 911 S 2.4 TdF oder dem 911 S 2.5 zu verdanken, die mit Hunderten von Siegen bei Rallyes und bei Rundstreckenrennen für den Mythos der Marke sorgten.

LE DÉBUT DE LA SAGA 911

Un an après la première mondiale au salon de Francfort, on y est : les premières 911 tant attendues sont livrées ; elles développent maintenant 130 CH de puissance et une vitesse maximale de 210 km/h. 235 exemplaires sont livrés jusqu'au 31 décembre 1964. Mais la 911, dont le prix de base atteint 21 900 Marks, est nettement plus chère que la 356 SC qui se vendait jusqu'en 1965 au prix de 16 500 Marks. C'est pourquoi la 912 fait son apparition dans la gamme en 1965. Elle allie la forme du nouveau coupé au moteur quatre cylindres développant une puissance de 90 CH de la 356 au prix de 16 250 Marks pour le modèle d'entrée de gamme. Et comme la demande pour une 911 cabriolet se fait de plus en plus pressante, la première Targa apparaît en 1966, à l'époque avec une vitre arrière en plastique rabattable, qui est remplacée dès 1969 par une vitre en verre. En 1969, la cylindrée passe à 2,2 litres, et à partir de 1971, une cylindrée de 2,4 litres assure jusqu'à 190 CH de puissance et 230 km/h pour la variante S. Dès le début, la 911 rencontre un vif succès dans le domaine du sport automobile grâce à des modèles limités tels que la 911 R, la 911 S 2.4 TdF ou la 911 S 2.5, qui remportent des centaines de victoires en rallye comme sur circuit et font naître le mythe de la marque.

Year of manufacture	1964
Engine capacity	1,991 cc
Power	130 hp / 96 kW
Transmission	five-speed transmission
Weight	1080 kg / 2,380 lbs.
Acceleration	0–100 km/h in 9.1 seconds
Top speed	210 km/h / 130 mph
Quantity produced	6,607 models

Year of manufacture	1965
Engine capacity	1,582 cc
Power	90 hp / 66 kW
Transmission	four-speed transmission
Weight	970 kg / 2,140 lbs.
Acceleration	0–100 km/h in 13.0 seconds
Top speed	185 km/h / 115 mph
Quantity produced	2,562 models

Year of manufacture	1966
Engine capacity	1,991 cc
Power	130 hp / 96 kW
Transmission	five-speed transmission
Weight	1080 kg / 2,380 lbs.
Acceleration	0–100 km/h in 9.1 seconds
Top speed	210 km/h / 130 mph
Quantity produced	236 models

Year of manufacture	1971
Engine capacity	2,341 cc
Power	190 hp / 140 kW
Transmission	five-speed transmission
Weight	1050 kg / 2,310 lbs.
Acceleration	0–100 km/h in 7.0 seconds
Top speed	230 km/h / 145 mph
Quantity produced	1,894 models

Year of manufacture	1967
Engine capacity	1,991 cc
Power	210 hp / 154 kW
Transmission	five-speed transmission
Weight	800 kg / 1,760 lbs.
Acceleration	not measured
Top speed	approx. 230 km/h / 145 mph
Quantity produced	19 models + 4 prototypes

Year of manufacture	1972
Engine capacity	2,466 cc
Power	270 hp / 199 kW
Transmission	five-speed transmission
Weight	960 kg / 2,120 lbs.
Acceleration	0–100 km/h in 5.6 seconds
Top speed	up to 250 km/h / 155 mph (depending on gear ratio)
Quantity produced	21 models

911 S 2.5 **1972**

THE "DUCKTAIL" MAKES THE DIFFERENCE

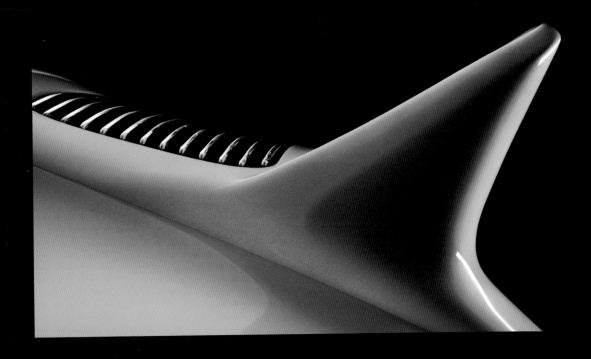

THE "DUCKTAIL" MAKES THE DIFFERENCE

Porsche had always been a company driven by motor sports—this was an area in which the company could make its mark and cultivate its image. The 911 had already earned the respect of its peers in 1967 with the 911 R; then, in 1973, came the Carrera RS, which opened up a new chapter to the story. No fewer than 500 homologation models had to be sold before the car could join the others in Group 4—and in the end the tally was 1,580 specimens that made the Carrera name famous all over the world. Beginning in 1974, from the first RSR 2.1 Turbo, the engineers in Zuffenhausen relied on supercharged engines—the 935/78 version of which delivered no less than 845 hp. This represented an explosion in engine power that had to be tamed by aspirated engines that were mandated by law beginning in 1978. The engine appeared in a number of racing versions that were very successful in rallies and captured numerous titles.

DER „ENTENBÜRZEL" SETZT ZEICHEN

Porsche war stets ein vom Motorsport getriebenes Unternehmen – hier konnte die Firma Zeichen setzen und fürs Image sorgen. Nachdem sich der 911 bereits 1967 als 911 R Respekt verschafft hatte, eröffnete der Carrera RS 1973 ein neues Kapitel. Nicht weniger als 500 Homologationsmodelle musste man verkaufen, um in der Gruppe 4 mitfahren zu können – letztlich sollten es 1580 Exemplare werden, die den Namen Carrera in alle Welt trugen. Ab 1974 setzte man in Zuffenhausen vom ersten RSR 2.1 Turbo an auf aufgeladene Triebwerke, die im Typ 935/78 nicht weniger als 845 PS ablieferten. Eine Leistungsexplosion, die von 1978 an reglementbedingt durch Saugmotoren zurückgefahren wurde und sich in einer Vielzahl von Rennvarianten niederschlug, die sehr erfolgreich bei Rallyes eingesetzt wurden und etliche Titel gewannen.

LA « QUEUE DE CANARD » SE DISTINGUE

Porsche a toujours été une entreprise motivée par le sport automobile ; c'est dans ce domaine qu'elle a pu se distinguer et assurer son image de marque. En 1967, la 911 avait suscité le respect dans sa version 911 R ; en 1973, la Carrera RS ouvre un nouveau chapitre. Il faut vendre pas moins de 500 modèles d'homologation pour pouvoir participer en groupe 4. Finalement, il s'en vend 1580 exemplaires, qui font connaître le nom de Carrera dans le monde entier. À partir de 1974, à Zuffenhausen, on parie dès la première RSR 2.1 turbo sur des motorisations turbocompressées qui fournissent pas moins de 845 CH pour le type 935/78. Une explosion de la performance qui, conformément à la réglementation, est réduite à partir de 1978 par l'utilisation de moteurs atmosphériques. Ces moteurs équipent alors un grand nombre de variantes sportives qui rencontrent un grand succès dans les rallyes et remportent d'innombrables titres.

Year of manufacture	1973
Engine capacity	2,687 cc
Power	210 hp / 154 kW
Transmission	five-speed transmission
Weight	1045 kg / 2,300 lbs.
Acceleration	0–100 km/h in 5.8 seconds
Top speed	245 km/h / 150 mph
Quantity produced	1,580 models

Year of manufacture	1973
Engine capacity	2,806 cc
Power	308 hp / 227 kW
Transmission	five-speed transmission
Weight	840 kg / 1,850 lbs.
Acceleration	0–100 km/h in 5.0 seconds
Top speed	280 km/h / 175 mph
Quantity produced	49 models

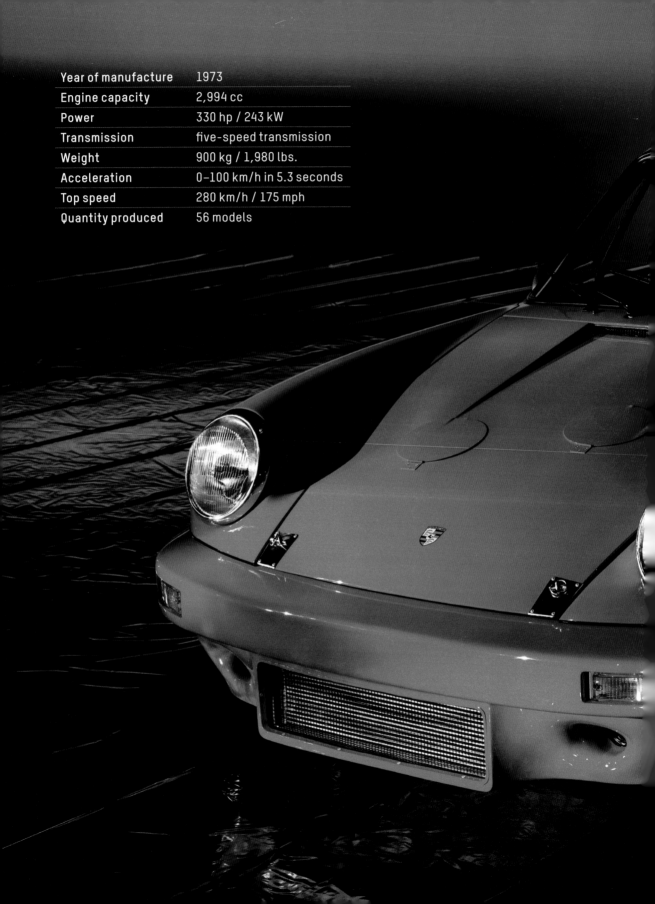

Year of manufacture	1973
Engine capacity	2,994 cc
Power	330 hp / 243 kW
Transmission	five-speed transmission
Weight	900 kg / 1,980 lbs.
Acceleration	0–100 km/h in 5.3 seconds
Top speed	280 km/h / 175 mph
Quantity produced	56 models

Year of manufacture	1974
Engine capacity	2,994 cc
Power	315 hp / 232 kW
Transmission	five-speed transmission
Weight	900 kg / 1,980 lbs.
Acceleration	0–100 km/h in 5.0 seconds
Top speed	250 km/h / 155 mph
Quantity produced	15 models

Year of manufacture	1974
Engine capacity	2,142 cc
Power	500 hp / 368 kW
Transmission	five-speed transmission
Weight	750 kg / 1,650 lbs.
Acceleration	not measured
Top speed	300 km/h / 185 mph
Quantity produced	4 models

Year of manufacture	1976
Engine capacity	2,994 cc
Power	485 hp / 357 kW
Transmission	four-speed transmission
Weight	1120 kg / 2,470 lbs.
Acceleration	not measured
Top speed	303 km/h / 190 mph
Quantity produced	44 models

Year of manufacture	1978
Engine capacity	3,211 cc
Power	845 hp / 622 kW
Transmission	four-speed transmission
Weight	1025 kg / 2,260 lbs.
Acceleration	not measured
Top speed	366 km/h / 225 mph
Quantity produced	1 model + 1 chassis

Year of manufacture	1978
Engine capacity	2,994 cc
Power	250 hp / 184 kW
Transmission	five-speed transmission
Weight	1180 kg / 2,600 lbs.
Acceleration	not measured
Top speed	228 km/h / 140 mph
Quantity produced	3 rally cars + 1 training car

Year of manufacture	1985
Engine capacity	2,996 cc
Power	255 hp / 188 kW (street version)
	300 hp / 221 kW (racing version)
Transmission	five-speed transmission
Weight	960 kg / 2,120 lbs.
Acceleration	0–100 km/h in
	5.0 seconds (street version)
	4.8 seconds (racing version)
Top speed	250 km/h / 155 mph
Quantity produced	21 models

911 ALL OVER THE WORLD

1973–1989

t had been ten years before Porsche made major revisions to the 11 in autumn of 1973—according to in-house records, this was the seventh model version so this series was dubbed the "G" model, after the seventh letter of the alphabet. By this time, all of the models offered a 2.7-liter engine, delivered between 150 and 210 hp of power and were available for delivery in coupé or Targa form. Visually speaking, the G model was easy to recognize by the accordion joints on the front and rear bumpers that—like the seats with built-in headrest and the padded dashboard—announced the desire for greater comfort and safety. In 1975 the engine capacity grew to 3 liters, and beginning in 1982 the series finally included a convertible, the Cabriolet, in addition to the Targa. The engine grew to 3.2 liters in 1983—and 1988 witnessed the advent of the Speedster, a limited-edition series of the most wide-open 11 of that era. And with the Carrera Clubsport, a sports version that was 220 lbs. lighter, for the first time Porsche again offered 340 buyers a basis for mass motor sports.

911 ALL OVER THE WORLD

Zehn Jahre waren vergangen, als Porsche im Herbst 1973 den Elfer deutlich überholte – intern zählte man die siebte Modellvariante, deshalb erhielt diese Baureihe die Bezeichnung G-Modell, nach dem siebten Buchstaben im Alphabet. Nun verfügten alle Modelle über 2,7 Liter Hubraum, leisteten zwischen 150 und 210 PS und waren als Coupé und als Targa lieferbar. Optisch war das G-Modell durch den Faltenbalg an der vorderen und hinteren Stoßstange zu erkennen, der – wie auch Sitze mit integrierter Nackenstütze und das gepolsterte Armaturenbrett – von dem Wunsch nach mehr Komfort und Sicherheit kündete. 1975 wuchs der Hubraum auf 3 Liter und von 1982 an war dann endlich auch zusätzlich zum Targa ein Cabriolet im Programm. 1983 wuchs der Hubraum dann auf 3,2 Liter – und 1988 folgte mit dem Speedster eine limitierte Serie des offensten Elfer der damaligen Jahre. Und mit dem Carrera Clubsport, einer um 100 Kilogramm erleichterten Sportversion, bot Porsche erstmals wieder 340 Käufern eine Basis für den Breitenmotorsport.

LA 911 FAIT LE TOUR DU MONDE

Dix ans se sont écoulés lorsque la société Porsche revisite clairement la 911 à l'automne 1973. En interne, on compte qu'il s'agit de la septième variante de ce modèle, c'est pourquoi cette série est appelée le modèle G comme la septième lettre de l'alphabet. Tous les modèles disposent dorénavant d'une cylindrée de 2,7 litres, d'une puissance comprise entre 150 et 210 CH et sont disponibles en version coupé et targa. Sur le plan esthétique, le modèle G est facilement reconnaissable au soufflet sur le pare-choc avant et le pare-choc arrière qui, tout comme les appuie-nuques intégrés aux sièges et le tableau de bord rembourré, sont les réponses au souhait de disposer de plus de confort et de sécurité. En 1975, la cylindrée atteint 3 litres et à partir de 1982, le programme comprend enfin une version cabriolet en plus de la version targa. En 1983, la cylindrée passe à 3,2 litres, et en 1988, une série limitée de la 911 la plus ouverte de l'époque est lancée, le Speedster. Enfin, avec la Carrera Clubsport, une version sport allégée de 100 kilogrammes, Porsche permet de nouveau, tout d'abord à 340 acheteurs, d'entrer dans le sport automobile de masse.

Magic flash
MF 900

Year of manufacture	1973
Engine capacity	2,687 cc
Power	150 hp / 110 kW
Transmission	five-speed transmission
Weight	1075 kg / 2,370 lbs.
Acceleration	0–100 km/h in 8.5 seconds
Top speed	210 km/h / 130 mph
Quantity produced	9,320 models

Year of manufacture	1975
Engine capacity	2,994 cc
Power	200 hp / 147 kW
Transmission	five-speed transmission
Weight	1120 kg / 2,470 lbs.
Acceleration	0–100 km/h in 6.3 seconds
Top speed	240 km/h / 150 mph
Quantity produced	1,083 models

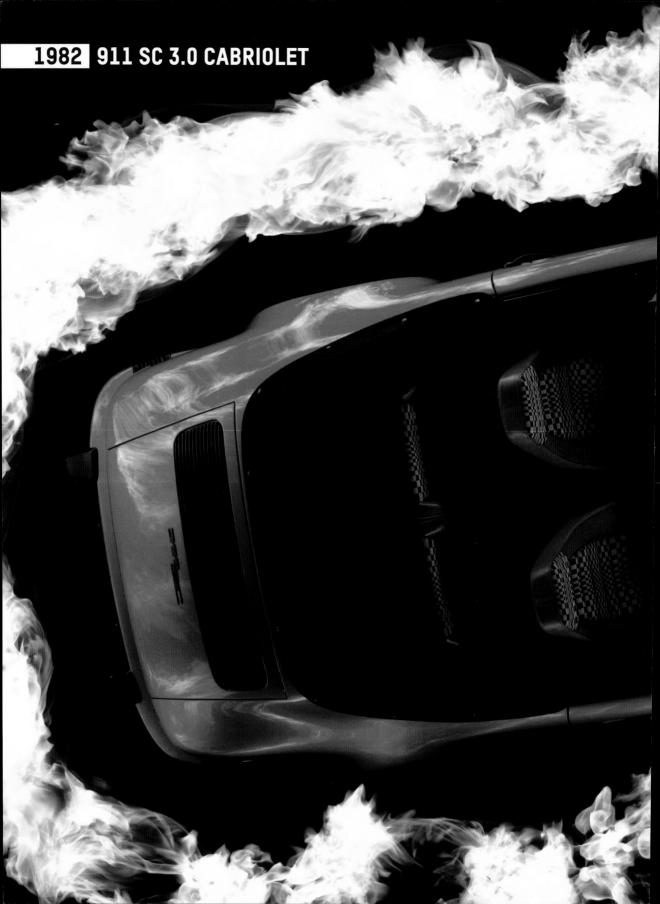

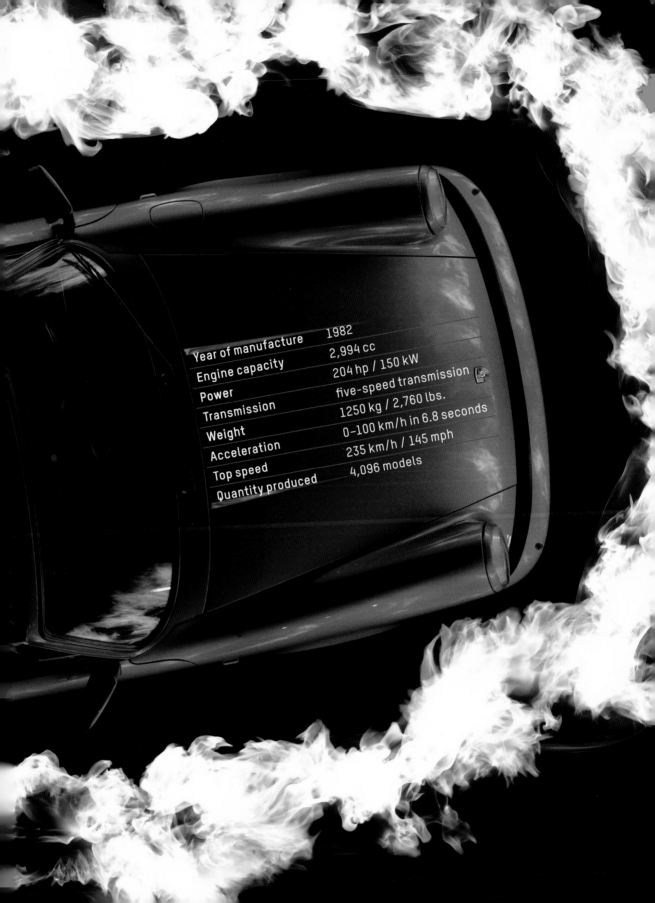

Year of manufacture	1982
Engine capacity	2,994 cc
Power	204 hp / 150 kW
Transmission	five-speed transmission
Weight	1250 kg / 2,760 lbs.
Acceleration	0–100 km/h in 6.8 seconds
Top speed	235 km/h / 145 mph
Quantity produced	4,096 models

Year of manufacture	1988
Engine capacity	3,164 cc
Power	231 hp / 170 kW
Transmission	five-speed transmission
Weight	1350 kg / 2,980 lbs.
Acceleration	0–100 km/h in 6.1 seconds
Top speed	240 km/h / 150 mph
Quantity produced	2,103 models

1987 911 CARRERA CLUBSPORT

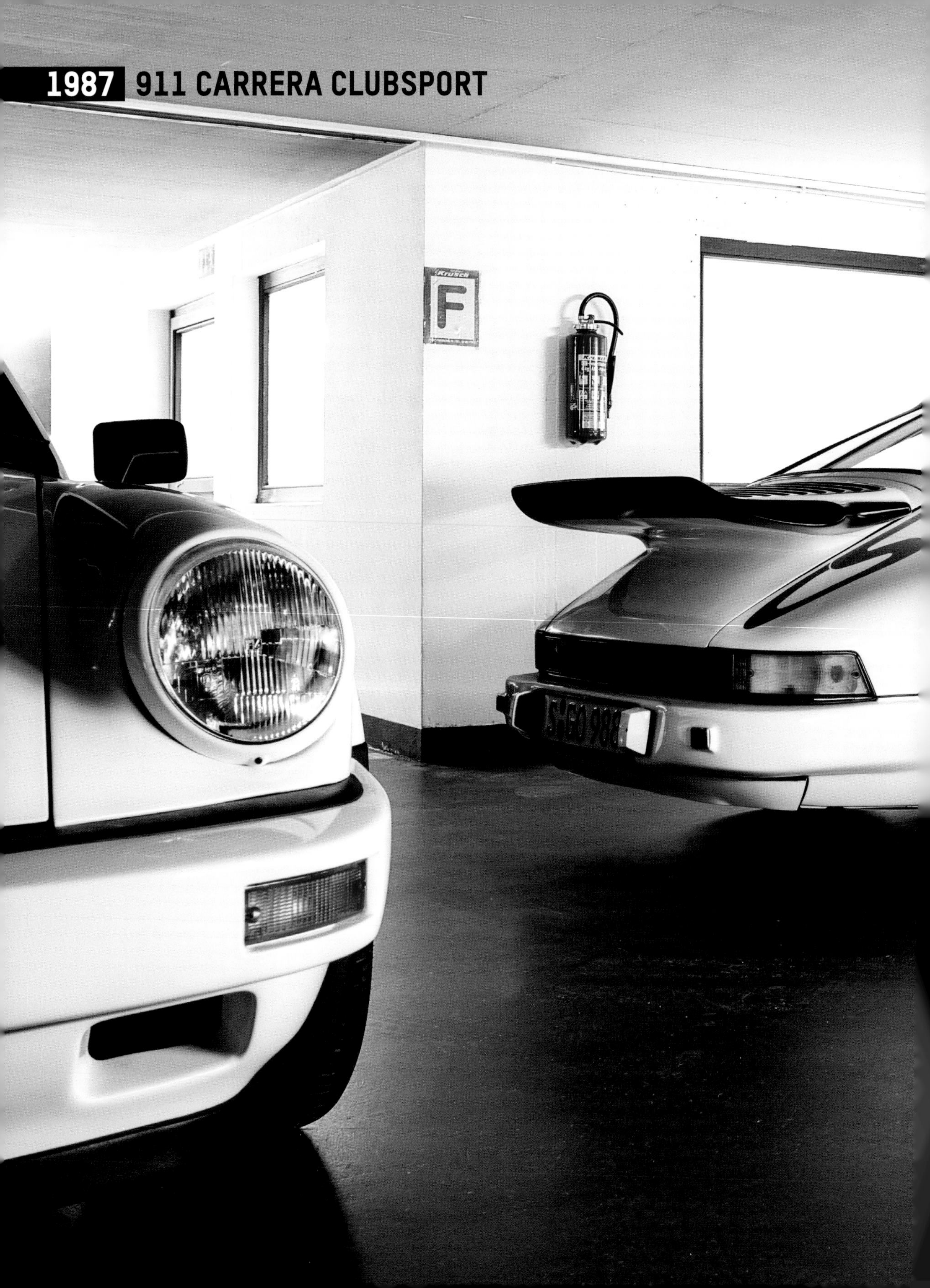

Year of manufacture	1987
Engine capacity	3,164 cc
Power	231 hp / 170 kW
Transmission	five-speed transmission
Weight	1150 kg / 2,540 lbs.
Acceleration	0–100 km/h in 6.1 seconds
Top speed	245 km/h / 150 mph
Quantity produced	340 models

Year of manufacture	1975
Engine capacity	2,994 cc
Power	260 hp / 191 kW
Transmission	four-speed transmission
Weight	1120 kg / 2,470 lbs.
Acceleration	0–100 km/h in 5.5 seconds
Top speed	250 km/h / 155 mph
Quantity produced	2,876 models

In autumn of 1974, Porsche presented the 911 Turbo 3.0, a version with 260 hp of power that—with the expertise of the turbo racing cars on board—combined extreme sportiness with comfort in a single car. 1977 brought the 300-hp version with the 3.3-liter engine that finally carried Porsche into the league of the super sports car manufacturers. This model remained in the program until 1988—with turbo versions of the Targa and Cabriolet also available for order between 1986 and 1988—although production levels of these models remained small: 297 Turbo Targas and 1,642 Turbo Cabriolets.

Im Herbst 1974 präsentierte Porsche mit dem 911 Turbo 3.0 dann eine 260 PS starke Variante, die – mit dem Know-how der Turbo-Rennwagen – extreme Sportlichkeit mit Komfort verband. 1977 folgte die 300 PS leistende Version mit 3,3 Litern Hubraum, die Porsche endgültig in die Liga der Super-Sportwagenhersteller führte. Dieses Modell sollte bis 1988 im Programm bleiben – wobei in den Jahren von 1986 bis 1988 noch der Targa und das Cabriolet als Turbo zu bestellen waren – allerdings blieb es hier bei kleinen Stückzahlen: 297 Turbo Targa und 1642 Turbo Cabriolets wurden gebaut.

À l'automne 1974, la maison Porsche présente une variante développant une puissance de 260 CH, la 911 turbo 3.0 qui, grâce au savoir-faire des voitures de course turbo, allie la sportivité extrême au confort. Puis en 1977 c'est une version de 300 CH et de 3,3 litres de cylindrée qui propulse la société Porsche définitivement dans la ligue des fabricants de super voitures de sport. Ce modèle restera au programme jusqu'en 1988, avec notamment la possibilité de commander une version targa et une version cabriolet du turbo de 1986 à 1988. Le nombre de voitures vendues reste cependant modeste : 297 turbo targa et 1642 turbo cabriolets.

Year of manufacture	1977
Engine capacity	3,299 cc
Power	300 hp / 221 kW
Transmission	four-speed transmission
Weight	1300 kg / 2,870 lbs.
Acceleration	0–100 km/h in 5.4 seconds
Top speed	260 km/h / 160 mph

Year of manufacture	1986
Engine capacity	3,299 cc
Power	300 hp / 221 kW
Transmission	four-speed transmission
Weight	1335 kg / 2,940 lbs.
Acceleration	0–100 km/h in 5.2 seconds
Top speed	260 km/h / 160 mph
Quantity produced	1,642 models (Cabriolet) / 297 models (Targa)

THE WORLD NEEDS ADVENTURE

1983–1988

THE WORLD NEEDS ADVENTURE

In the early 1980s, when the Fédération Internationale de l'Automobile (FIA) required just 200 built basic models for homologation for Group B, Porsche also decided to develop a top model that offered unprecedented power along with all of the features that were technically feasible at the time. The result was the 959, a model with a 2.85-liter, six-cylinder, sequentially turbocharged engine featuring two parallel KKK turbochargers, offering 450 hp and an elaborate four-wheel drive. 37 prototype pilot models of the 959 were built in 1985, followed by 255 Komfort and 37 Sport versions of the car in 1987 and 1988. Porsche then built another eight Komfort models from spare parts in 1992. The car made race appearances, too: In 1986 the 959 won the Paris-Dakar Rally, and in Le Mans the 961 (based on the 959) registered a class victory and came in seventh place in the overall classification.

DIE WELT BRAUCHT ABENTEUER

Als die Fédération Internationale de l'Automobile (FIA) Anfang der 1980er Jahre für die Homologation für die Gruppe B nur noch 200 gebaute Basismodelle forderte, entschloss sich auch Porsche, ein Topmodell mit nie gesehener Leistung und mit allen technisch darstellbaren Features zu entwickeln. Das Ergebnis war der 959, der mit einem 2,85 Liter großen Sechszylinder und einer Registeraufladung mit zwei parallel geschalteten KKK-Turboladern 450 PS über einen aufwändigen Allradantrieb auf die Straße brachte. Von dem 959 entstanden 1985 37 Prototypen und Vorserien-Fahrzeuge, denen 1987 und 1988 dann 255 Komfort- und 37 Sport-Versionen folgten. 1992 baute Porsche dann aus Ersatzteilen weitere acht Komfort-Modelle auf. Der Wagen kam auch bei Rennen zum Einsatz: 1986 gewann der 959 die Rallye Paris-Dakar, während der auf dem 959 basierende 961 in Le Mans einen Klassensieg erreichte und im Gesamtklassement Siebter wurde.

LE MONDE A BESOIN D'AVENTURE

Lorsqu'au début des années 80, la Fédération Internationale de l'Automobile (FIA) revoit à la baisse ses exigences pour l'homologation pour le groupe B et n'exige plus que la construction de 200 modèles de base, Porsche décide de développer à son tour un top modèle qui présente des performances encore jamais vues et toutes les caractéristiques techniques imaginables. C'est ainsi que naît la 959 qui, équipée d'un six cylindres de 2,85 litres et d'une suralimentation assurée par deux turbocompresseurs KKK montés en parallèle, développe 450 CH par l'intermédiaire d'une transmission intégrale complexe. En 1985, la 959 compte 37 prototypes et véhicules de présérie, suivis en 1987 et 1988 de 255 versions confort et 37 versions sport. En 1992, Porsche construit huit nouveaux modèles confort à partir de pièces détachées. La voiture participe également à des courses : en 1986, la 959 remporte le rallye Paris-Dakar, tandis que la 961, qui reprend la base de la 959, remporte au Mans une victoire dans sa catégorie et une septième place au classement général.

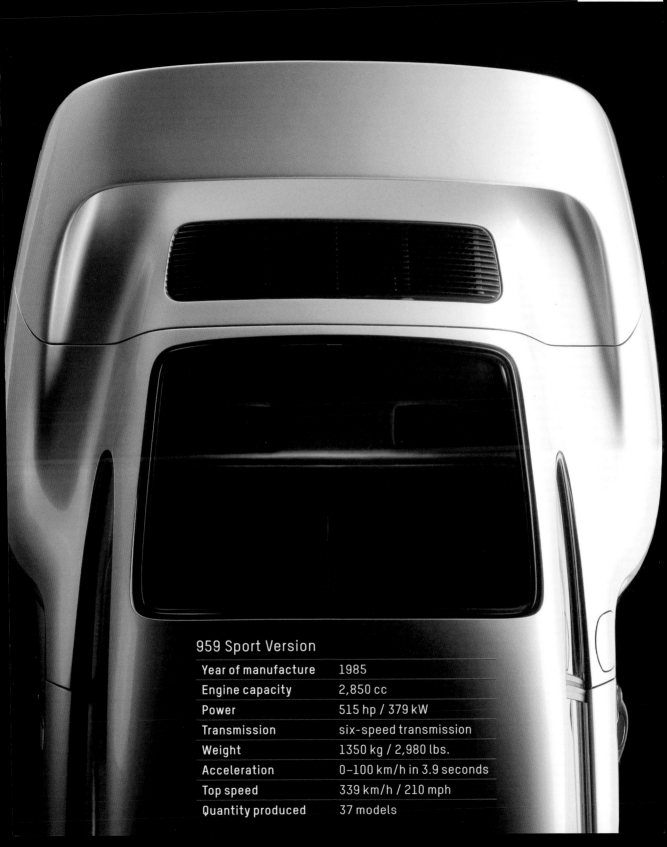

959 Sport Version

Year of manufacture	1985
Engine capacity	2,850 cc
Power	515 hp / 379 kW
Transmission	six-speed transmission
Weight	1350 kg / 2,980 lbs.
Acceleration	0–100 km/h in 3.9 seconds
Top speed	339 km/h / 210 mph
Quantity produced	37 models

Year of manufacture	1985
Engine capacity	2,850 cc
Power	450 hp / 331 kW
Transmission	six-speed transmission
Weight	1450 kg / 3,200 lbs.
Acceleration	0–100 km/h in 3.9 seconds
Top speed	over 315 km/h / 195 mph
Quantity produced	263 models + 37 prototypes and pilot models

STILL AIR-COOLED

1988–1997

STILL AIR-COOLED

The 1980s were not an easy time for Porsche. In fact, some members of the Executive Board thought the 11 was a phase-out model. More attention was paid to the 924, 928, 944 and 968 model series, while the 911 was reduced to model facelifts. Then, in 1988—late, but not too late—the 964 was issued, a new 11 generation offered for the first time as a Carrera 4 with four-wheel drive. Along with a new 3.6-liter engine with 250 hp, the model now came with ABS, power steering and airbags as standard features for the first time. The line was quickly supplemented by the Targa and a Cabriolet, while the spartan Speedster was issued, from 1992 on, in a limited edition of 930 cars. From 1990 on, the Turbo—and from 1991 the Turbo S as well—provided better driving performance, and beginning in 1991 the emphatically sporty Carrera RS was also available in very small quantities.

NOCH KÜHLT DIE LUFT

Porsche hatte in den 1980er Jahren keine einfache Zeit: Teile des Vorstands glaubten, dass der Elfer ein Auslaufmodell sei. Man kümmerte sich stärker um die Modellreihen 924, 928, 944 und 968, während der 911 nur Modellpflegemaßnahmen erhielt. Spät, aber nicht zu spät, erschien dann 1988 mit dem Typ 964 eine neue Elfer-Generation, die erstmals als Carrera 4 mit Allradantrieb angeboten wurde. Neben einem neuen 3,6-Liter-Motor mit 250 PS kamen zudem ABS, Servolenkung und Airbags serienmäßig zum Einsatz. Rasch ergänzten der Targa und ein Cabriolet das Programm, *während der spartanische Speedster ab 1992 in einer auf 930 Exemplare limitierten Serie erschien. Von 1990 an sorgte der Turbo – und von 1991 an auch der Turbo S – für noch bessere Fahrleistungen, und ab 1991 war auch der betont sportliche Carrera RS in kleinsten Stückzahlen lieferbar.*

LE DERNIER MODÈLE À REFROIDISSEMENT À AIR

Les années 80 ne sont pas évidentes pour la maison Porsche : certains membres de la direction croient que la 911 est un modèle qui a fait son temps. On reporte donc davantage l'attention sur les séries 924, 928, 944 et 968, tandis que la 911 ne bénéficie que de mesures d'entretien. Ce n'est que tard, bien qu'heureusement pas encore trop tard, en 1988, qu'une nouvelle génération du modèle 911 apparaît la 964, qui est proposée pour la première fois en version Carrera 4 avec traction à quatre roues motrices. Outre un nouveau moteur de 3,6 litres de cylindrée et 250 CH de puissance, la 964 bénéficie pour la première fois du système ABS, de la direction assistée et d'airbags en série. Une version targa et un cabriolet viennent rapidement compléter la gamme, tandis qu'une série limitée à 930 exemplaires du spartiate Speedster apparaît en 1992. À partir de 1990, le modèle turbo, et dès 1991 le turbo S, offrent des performances de conduite encore meilleures, et à partir de 1991, c'est au tour de la franchement sportive Carrera RS de faire son apparition en très petit nombre.

Year of manufacture	1988
Engine capacity	3,600 cc
Power	250 hp / 184 kW
Transmission	five-speed transmission/ four-wheel drive
Weight	1450 kg / 3,200 lbs.
Acceleration	0–100 km/h in 5.7 seconds
Top speed	260 km/h / 160 mph
Quantity produced	19,484 models

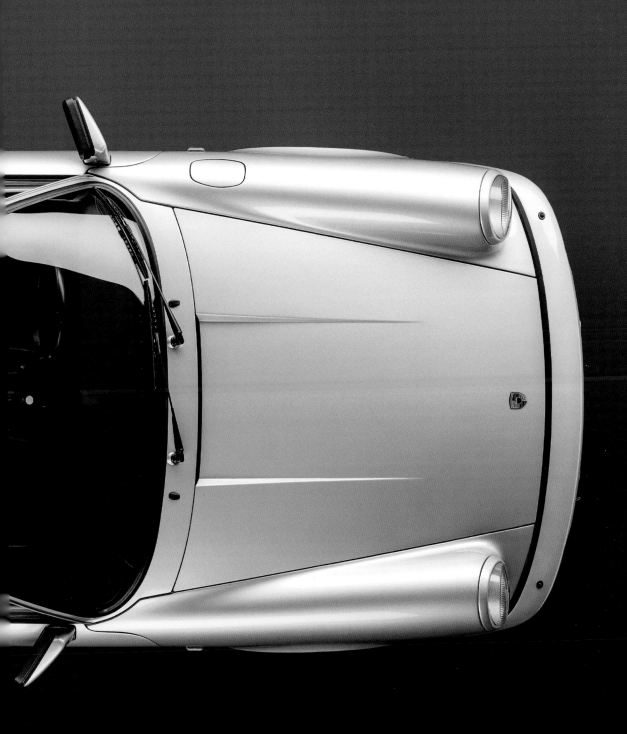

Year of manufacture	1990
Engine capacity	3,299 cc
Power	320 hp / 235 kW
Transmission	five-speed transmission
Weight	1470 kg / 3,240 lbs.
Acceleration	0–100 km/h in 5.0 seconds
Top speed	270 km/h / 170 mph
Quantity produced	3,660 models

Year of manufacture	1991
Engine capacity	3,299 cc
Power	381 hp / 280 kW
Transmission	five-speed transmission
Weight	1290 kg / 2,840 lbs.
Acceleration	0–100 km/h in 4.7 seconds
Top speed	290 km/h / 180 mph
Quantity produced	86 models

Year of manufacture	1993
Engine capacity	3,598 cc
Power	360 hp / 265 kW
Transmission	five-speed transmission
Weight	1470 kg / 3,240 lbs.
Acceleration	0–100 km/h in 4.8 seconds
Top speed	280 km/h / 175 mph
Quantity produced	1,422 models (+ 14 Cabriolets)

Year of manufacture	1992
Engine capacity	3,600 cc
Power	260 hp / 191 kW
Transmission	five-speed transmission
Weight	1220 kg / 2,690 lbs.
Acceleration	0–100 km/h in 5.3 seconds
Top speed	260 km/h / 160 mph
Quantity produced	1,280 models

Year of manufacture	1993
Engine capacity	3,600 cc
Power	250 hp / 184 kW
Transmission	five-speed transmission
Weight	1450 kg / 3,200 lbs.
Acceleration	0–100 km/h in 5.7 seconds
Top speed	260 km/h / 160 mph
Quantity produced	911 models

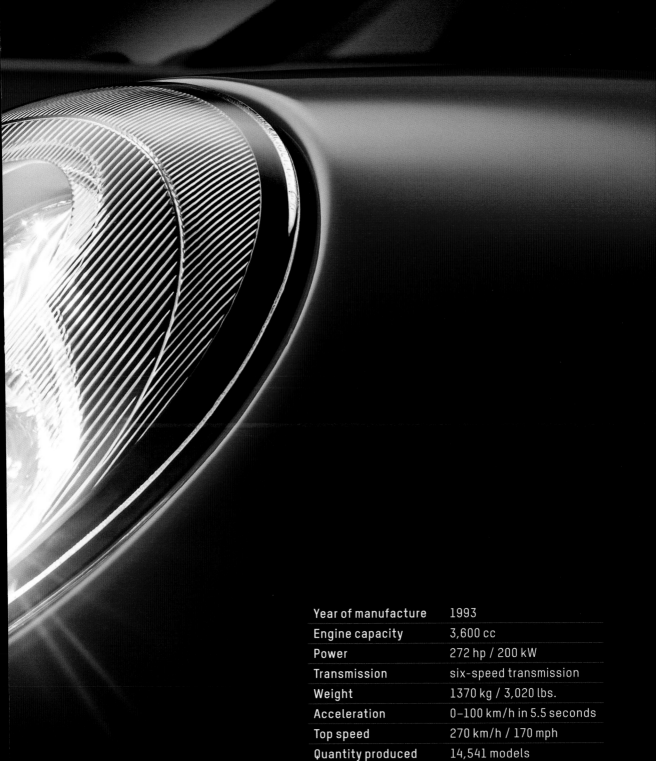

Year of manufacture	1993
Engine capacity	3,600 cc
Power	272 hp / 200 kW
Transmission	six-speed transmission
Weight	1370 kg / 3,020 lbs.
Acceleration	0–100 km/h in 5.5 seconds
Top speed	270 km/h / 170 mph
Quantity produced	14,541 models

In September 1993, to mark the 30th birthday of the 11 series, Porsche presented the newly revised classic, a model referred to in-house by its code name: 993. In terms of its appearance, the fact that the car's new aerodynamic, elliptical headlights had been gently integrated in the fenders was a demonstration that the topic of drag had gained in importance. At the same time, the technicians had given the car's body significantly higher torsional rigidity—without any added weight. From the beginning, the Coupé and Cabriolet were equipped with rear-wheel or four-wheel drive and a 272-hp engine. In 1995, dealers took delivery of the new Targa with its spacious glass roof, along with the 408-hp-strong Turbo, which was later followed by the Turbo S with up to 450 hp. The 300-hp Carrera RS was available for only two years, a vehicle that quickly commanded respect on the racetrack.

Im September 1993 präsentierte Porsche – zum 30. Geburtstag der Elfer-Baureihe – den erneut überarbeiteten Klassiker, der intern den Codenamen 993 trug. Äußerlich zeigten die neuen, aerodynamisch sanft in den Kotflügel integrierten Ellipsoid-Scheinwerfer, dass das Thema Luftwiderstand an Bedeutung gewonnen hatte, während die Techniker der Karosserie eine deutlich höhere Verwindungssteifigkeit mit auf den Weg gegeben hatten – bei gleichem Gewicht. Coupé und Cabriolet waren von Anfang an mit Heck- oder Allradantrieb und 272 PS ausgestattet. 1995 kam der neue Targa mit seinem großen Glasdach zu den Händlern, ebenso wie der 408 PS starke Turbo, dem später noch der Turbo S mit bis zu 450 PS folgte. Nur zwei Jahre lang war der Carrera RS mit 300 PS zu haben, der sich rasch auf den Rennstrecken Respekt verschaffen konnte.

En septembre 1993, à l'occasion du 30ème anniversaire de la série 911, la maison Porsche présente le classique revisité, qui porte en interne le nom de code 993. Sur le plan extérieur, les nouveaux phares ellipsoïdes aérodynamiques intégrés tout en douceur aux ailes sont le signe que l'aérodynamique est un sujet qui a gagné en importance, tandis que les techniciens parviennent à fortement augmenter la résistance à la torsion de la carrosserie pour un poids constant. Les versions coupé et cabriolet sont équipées dès le début d'une traction arrière ou d'une traction à quatre roues motrices et d'une puissance de 272 CH. En 1995, la nouvelle version targa avec son grand toit de verre fait son apparition chez les concessionnaires, de même que la version turbo et ses 408 CH, suivie un peu plus tard par la version turbo S qui affiche jusqu'à 450 CH. La Carrera RS et ses 300 CH, qui n'est disponible que pendant deux ans, impose très vite le respect sur les circuits.

911 TARGA (993) 1995

Year of manufacture	1995
Engine capacity	3,600 cc
Power	285 hp / 210 kW
Transmission	six-speed transmission
Weight	1400 kg / 3,090 lbs.
Acceleration	0–100 km/h in 5.5 seconds
Top speed	277 km/h / 170 mph
Quantity produced	4,583 models

Year of manufacture	1995
Engine capacity	3,600 cc
Power	408 hp / 300 kW
Transmission	six-speed transmission / four-wheel drive
Weight	1500 kg / 3,310 lbs.
Acceleration	0–100 km/h in 4.5 seconds
Top speed	290 km/h / 180 mph
Quantity produced	5,978 models

Year of manufacture	1995
Engine capacity	3,746 cc
Power	300 hp / 221 kW
Transmission	six-speed transmission / rear-wheel drive
Weight	1270 kg / 2,800 lbs.
Acceleration	0–100 km/h in 5.0 seconds
Top speed	277 km/h / 170 mph
Quantity produced	1,146 models

CALLING THE WORLD'S RACETRACKS HOME

1990–2010

CALLING THE WORLD'S RACETRACKS HOME

In 1987, 340 customers with an interest in mass racing sports took delivery of the Clubsport, a variation of the Carrera that was lighter by 220 lbs. The success of this model led to the introduction of the Porsche Carrera Cup, an event that from 1990 on replaced the Porsche 944 Turbo Cup, which had previously been the brand cup. For this race, the 997 GT3 Cup car was built, a model later followed by further elaborations of the same version. Today's spectacular racing series, the Porsche Carrera Cup and the Porsche Supercup, are held around the world with the 450-hp 911 GT3 Cup. Parallel to this, on the basis of the GT2 and GT3 models, Porsche has also produced RS and RSR models for major racing events such as Le Mans. The most extreme version was the 911 GT1, entered in 1997, which with its water-cooled mid-engine was comparable to the 911 only up to a point and celebrated a twin victory in Le Mans in 1998. In 2010, Porsche surprised the automotive world with the 911 GT3 R Hybrid (997) racing car.

AUF DEN RENNSTRECKEN ZU HAUSE

1987 erhielten 340 am Breitenmotorsport interessierte Kunden mit dem Clubsport eine um 100 Kilogramm leichtere Carrera-Variante. Deren Erfolg führte zur Einführung des Porsche Carrera Cups, der von 1990 an den Porsche 944 Turbo Cup als Markenpokal ablöste. Für diesen wurde der 997 GT3 Cup-Wagen gebaut, dem in den darauffolgenden Jahren weiterentwickelte Versionen folgten. Heute finden die spektakulären Rennserien des Porsche Carrera Cup und des Porsche Supercup rund um die Welt mit dem 450 PS starken 911 GT3 Cup statt. Parallel dazu hat Porsche auf der Basis der GT2- und GT3-Modelle auch RS- und RSR-Modelle für die großen Rennen wie Le Mans produziert. Die extremste Version war der 1997 eingesetzte 911 GT1, der mit seinem wassergekühlten Mittelmotor nur noch bedingt mit dem 911 vergleichbar war und 1998 in Le Mans einen Doppelsieg feiern konnte. 2010 überraschte Porsche mit dem Rennwagen 911 GT3 R Hybrid (997).

À L'AISE SUR LES CIRCUITS

En 1987, 340 clients intéressés par le sport automobile de masse se voient proposer la Clubsport, une variante Carrera plus légère d'une centaine de kilogrammes. Son succès conduit à l'introduction du championnat monotype Porsche Carrera Cup, qui succède à partir de 1990 à la Porsche 944 Turbo Cup. C'est pour elle que le modèle 997 GT3 Cup est construit, qui donne plusieurs versions améliorées au cours des années suivantes. Aujourd'hui, les courses spectaculaires de la Porsche Carrera Cup et de la Porsche Supercup se déroulent dans le monde entier avec le modèle 911 GT3 Cup d'une puissance de 450 CH. En parallèle, la maison Porsche produit également des modèles RS et RSR sur la base des modèles GT2 et GT3 pour de grandes courses telles que Le Mans. La version la plus extrême est le modèle 911 GT1 qui entre en piste en 1997, un modèle équipé d'un moteur à refroidissement à eau qui n'a plus grand chose à voir avec la 911 et qui remporte une double victoire en 1998 au Mans. En 2010, la maison Porsche surprend tout le monde avec sa voiture de course hybride, la 911 GT3 R (997).

911 GT1 (Racing Version)

Year of manufacture	1997
Engine capacity	3,200 cc
Power	600 hp / 441 kW
Transmission	six-speed transmission
Weight	1050 kg / 2,310 lbs.
Acceleration	not measured
Top speed	approx. 320 km/h / 200 mph
Quantity produced	10 models

911 GT1 (Street Version)

Year of manufacture	1998
Engine capacity	3,164 cc
Power	544 hp / 400 kW
Transmission	six-speed transmission
Weight	approx. 1120 kg / 2,470 lbs.
Acceleration	0–100 km/h in 3.7 seconds
Top speed	310 km/h / 195 mph
Quantity produced	21 models

Year of manufacture	1990
Engine capacity	3,598 cc
Power	265 hp / 195 kW
Transmission	five-speed transmission
Weight	1210 kg / 2,670 lbs.
Acceleration	not measured
Top speed	270 km/h / 170 mph
Quantity produced	50 models

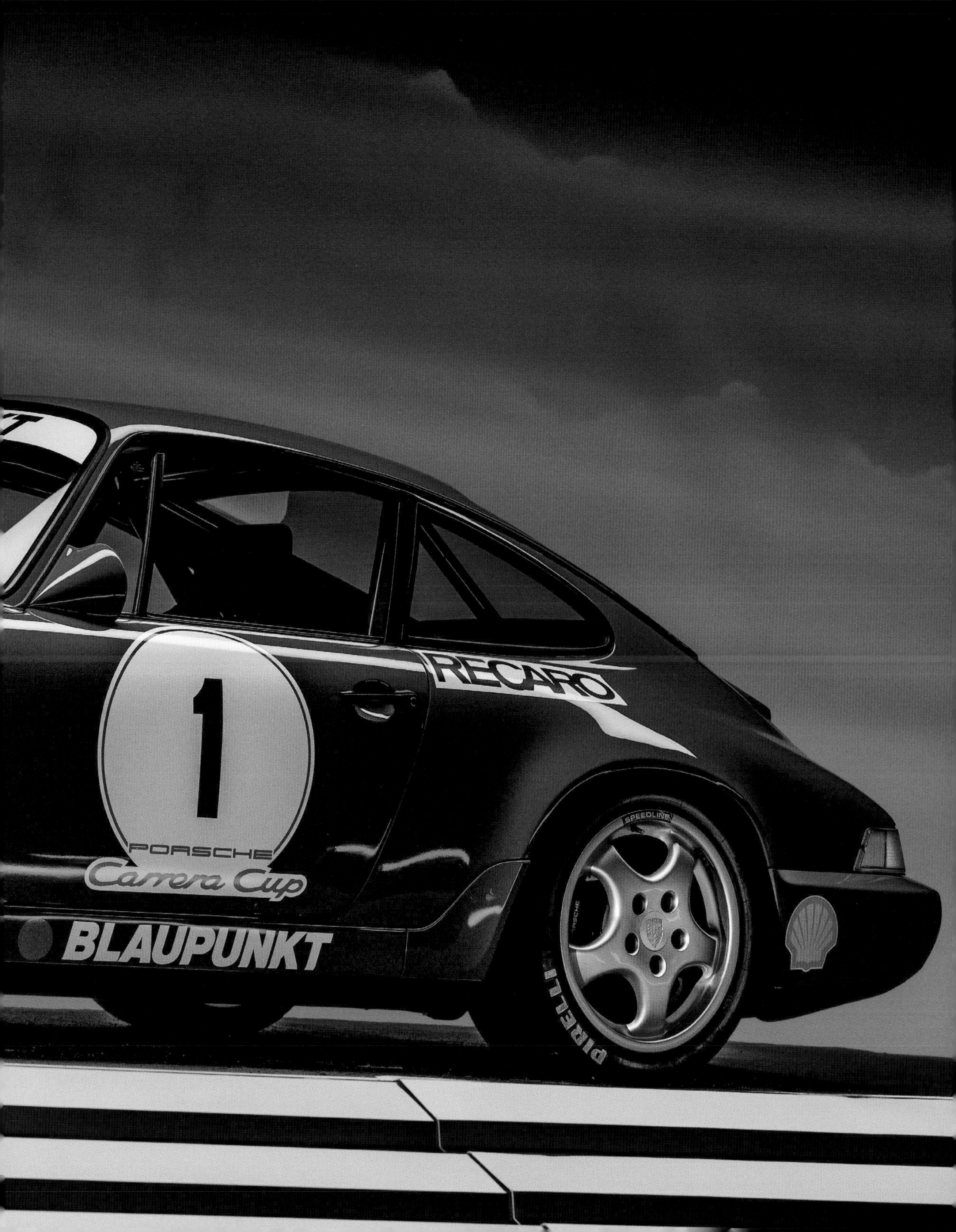
1
PORSCHE
Carrera Cup
RECARO
BLAUPUNKT
SPEEDLINE
PIRELLI

Year of manufacture	1993
Engine capacity	3,164 cc
Power	475 hp / 349 kW
Transmission	five-speed transmission
Weight	1000 kg / 2,200 lbs.
Acceleration	not measured
Top speed	306 km/h / 190 mph
Quantity produced	1 model

Year of manufacture	1994
Engine capacity	3,746 cc
Power	315 hp / 232 kW
Transmission	six-speed transmission
Weight	1120 kg / 2,470 lbs.
Acceleration	not measured
Top speed	280 km/h / 175 mph
Quantity produced	40 models

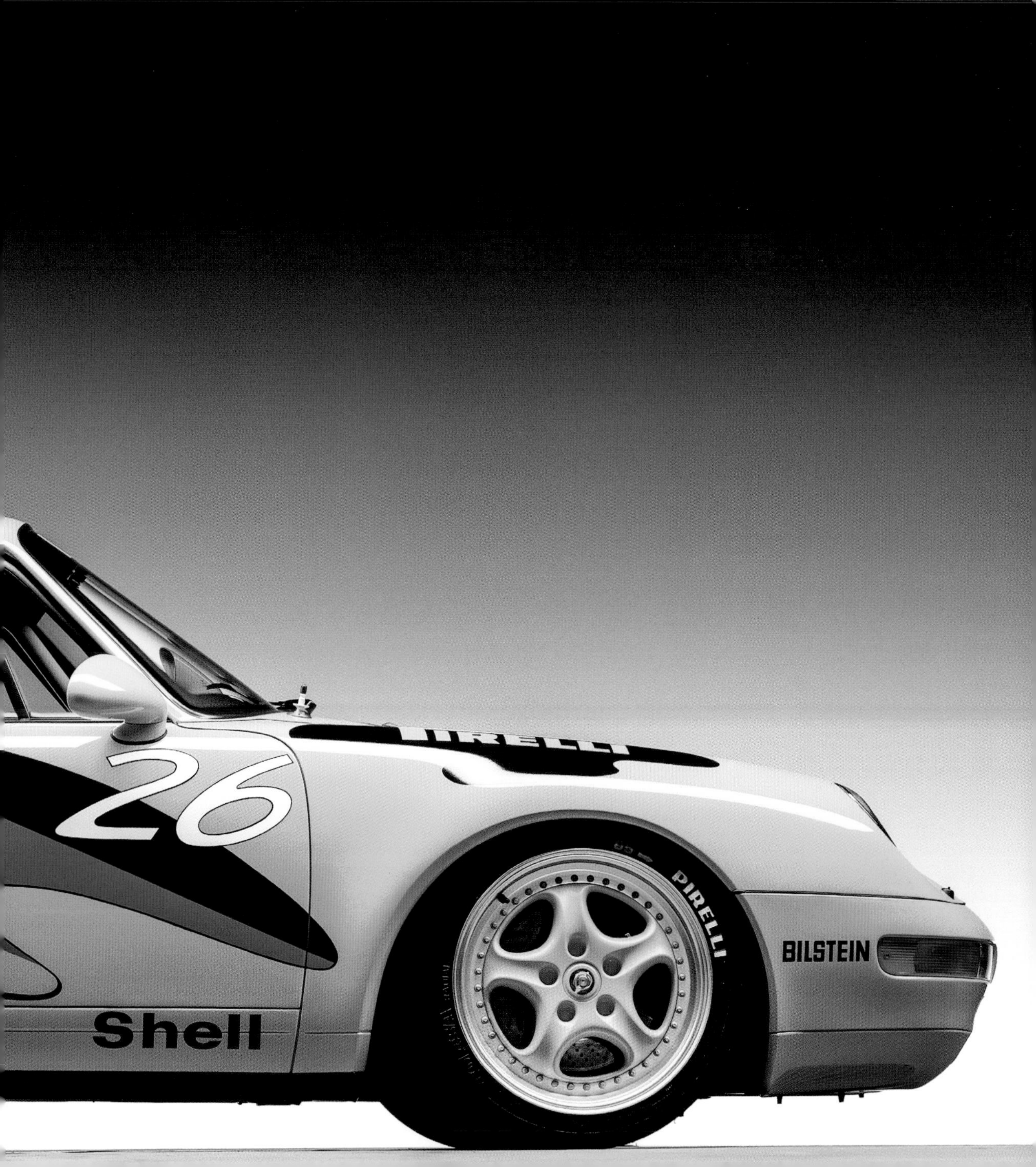
PIRELLI
26
PIRELLI
BILSTEIN
Shell

Year of manufacture	1995
Engine capacity	3,598 cc
Power	600 hp / 441 kW
Transmission	six-speed transmission
Weight	1100 kg / 2,430 lbs.
Acceleration	not measured
Top speed	310 km/h / 195 mph
Quantity produced	8 models

Year of manufacture	1996
Engine capacity	3,746 cc
Power	315 hp / 232 kW
Transmission	six-speed transmission
Weight	1120 kg / 2,470 lbs.
Acceleration	not measured
Top speed	308 km/h / 190 mph
Quantity produced	54 models

Year of manufacture	1998
Engine capacity	3,598 cc
Power	360 hp / 265 kW
Transmission	six-speed transmission
Weight	1140 kg / 2,510 lbs.
Acceleration	not measured
Top speed	286 km/h / 180 mph
Quantity produced	30 models

Year of manufacture	2001
Engine capacity	3,598 cc
Power	360 hp / 265 kW
Transmission	six-speed transmission
Weight	1350 kg / 2,980 lbs.
Acceleration	not measured
Top speed	308 km/h / 190 mph
Quantity produced	51 models

Year of manufacture	2004
Engine capacity	3,598 cc
Power	390 hp / 287 kW
Transmission	six-speed transmission
Weight	1150 kg / 2,540 lbs.
Acceleration	not measured
Top speed	308 km/h / 190 mph
Quantity produced	150 models

Year of manufacture	2010
Engine capacity	3,996 cc
Power	480 hp / 353 kW
Transmission	six-speed transmission / four-wheel drive
Weight	1200 kg / 2,650 lbs.
Acceleration	not measured
Top speed	308 km/h / 190 mph
Quantity produced	1 model

THE ENVIRONMENT BECKONS

1997–2012

THE ENVIRONMENT BECKONS

The demands on automobiles have changed dramatically since 1963: while there was little interest in safety or environmental regulations back then, today electronics, driver-assist systems and catalytic converters provide optimal protection, low fuel consumption and the best possible emissions levels. To meet the statutory requirements, in 1997 Porsche began cooling the hitherto air-cooled six-cylinder engine with water—the uproar was great enough for some to claim that the new 996 series was no longer a genuine Porsche 911. But the newcomer carried the day: the completely revised and larger 11 was available as a Coupé, Targa and Cabriolet, with rear- or four-wheel drive. Then, in 2000, came the Turbo, and the sportier drivers could turn to the GT2 and GT3 versions, or to the Clubsport versions that made do without electronic driver-assistance features. 2004 marked the transition to the more visually than technologically revised 997. The climax and terminus of the series was the 911 GT3 RS 4.0.

DIE UMWELT RUFT UND FORDERT

Seit 1963 verändern sich die Anforderungen an Automobile dramatisch: Waren damals Sicherheit und Umweltvorschriften wenig gefragt, so sorgen heute Elektronik, Fahrerassistenten und Katalysatoren für optimalen Schutz, niedrige Verbrauchs- und beste Abgaswerte. Um die gesetzlichen Vorgaben zu erfüllen, begann Porsche 1997 die bislang luftgekühlten Sechszylinder mit Wasser zu kühlen – entsprechend groß war die Aufregung, dass die neue 996-Baureihe kein echter Porsche 911 mehr sei. Doch natürlich überzeugte auch der Neue: Der komplett überarbeitete und größer gewordene Elfer war als Coupé, Targa und Cabriolet mit Heck- oder Allradantrieb zu haben, 2000 kam dann der Turbo,

und die sportlicheren Fahrer konnten zu der GT2- und GT3-Varianten greifen oder zu den Clubsport-Versionen, die auf elektronische Fahrhilfen verzichteten. 2004 erfolgte der Übergang zum mehr optisch als technisch überarbeiteten 997. Höhe- und Schlusspunkt der Baureihe war der 911 GT3 RS 4.0.

L'ENVIRONNEMENT DEVIENT UNE EXIGENCE IMPORTANTE

Depuis 1963, les exigences vis-à-vis de l'automobile ont considérablement changé : tandis qu'autrefois, la sécurité et la réglementation en matière de protection de l'environnement ne jouaient quasiment aucun rôle, aujourd'hui l'électronique, les assistants de conduite et les catalyseurs assurent une protection optimale et de faibles valeurs de consommation et de rejets de gaz. Afin de répondre aux directives de la loi, la maison Porsche commence en 1997 à refroidir à l'eau ses six cylindres refroidis jusqu'alors à l'air, ce qui suscite une vive émotion et fait courir le bruit que la nouvelle série 996 n'est plus une vraie Porsche 911. Mais naturellement, la petite nouvelle ne met pas longtemps à convaincre elle aussi cette 911 complètement revisitée et agrandie est disponible en version coupé, targa et cabriolet avec traction arrière ou traction à quatre roues motrices. En 2000, c'est au tour du turbo de faire son apparition, et les plus sportifs parmi la clientèle peuvent choisir les variantes GT2 et GT3 ou l'une des versions Clubsport, qui renoncent à toute assistance de conduite. En 2004, c'est le passage à la 997, qui subit davantage des modifications sur le plan esthétique que technique. Le dernier et le plus abouti des modèles de la série est le 911 GT3 RS 4.0.

Year of manufacture	1997
Engine capacity	3,387 cc
Power	300 hp / 221 kW
Transmission	six-speed transmission
Weight	1320 kg / 2,910 lbs.
Acceleration	0–100 km/h in 5.2 seconds
Top speed	280 km/h / 175 mph
Quantity produced	54,733 models

Year of manufacture	2000
Engine capacity	3,600 cc
Power	420 hp / 309 kW
Transmission	six-speed transmission
Weight	1495 kg / 3,300 lbs.
Acceleration	0–100 km/h in 4.2 seconds
Top speed	305 km/h / 190 mph
Quantity produced	22,062 models

Year of manufacture	2001
Engine capacity	3,600 cc
Power	462 hp / 340 kW
Transmission	six-speed transmission
Weight	1495 kg / 3,300 lbs.
Acceleration	0–100 km/h in 4.1 seconds
Top speed	315 km/h / 195 mph
Quantity produced	963 models

Year of manufacture	2004
Engine capacity	3,596 cc
Power	325 hp / 239 kW
Transmission	six-speed transmission
Weight	1490 kg / 3,280 lbs.
Acceleration	0–100 km/h in 5.0 seconds
Top speed	285 km/h / 175 mph
Quantity produced	25,770 models

Year of manufacture	2006
Engine capacity	3,824 cc
Power	355 hp / 261 kW
Transmission	six-speed transmission / four-wheel drive
Weight	1450 kg / 3,200 lbs.
Acceleration	0–100 km/h in 4.8 seconds
Top speed	288 km/h / 180 mph
Quantity produced	3,328 models

targa 4S

Year of manufacture	2006
Engine capacity	3,600 cc
Power	480 hp / 353 kW
Transmission	six-speed transmission
Weight	1450 kg / 3,200 lbs.
Acceleration	0–100 km/h in 3.9 seconds
Top speed	310 km/h / 195 mph
Quantity produced	14,298 models

Engine capacity	3,600 cc
Power	415 hp / 305 kW
Transmission	six-speed transmission
Weight	1395 kg / 3,080 lbs.
Acceleration	0–100 km/h in 4.3 seconds
Top speed	310 km/h / 195 mph
Quantity produced	3,329 models

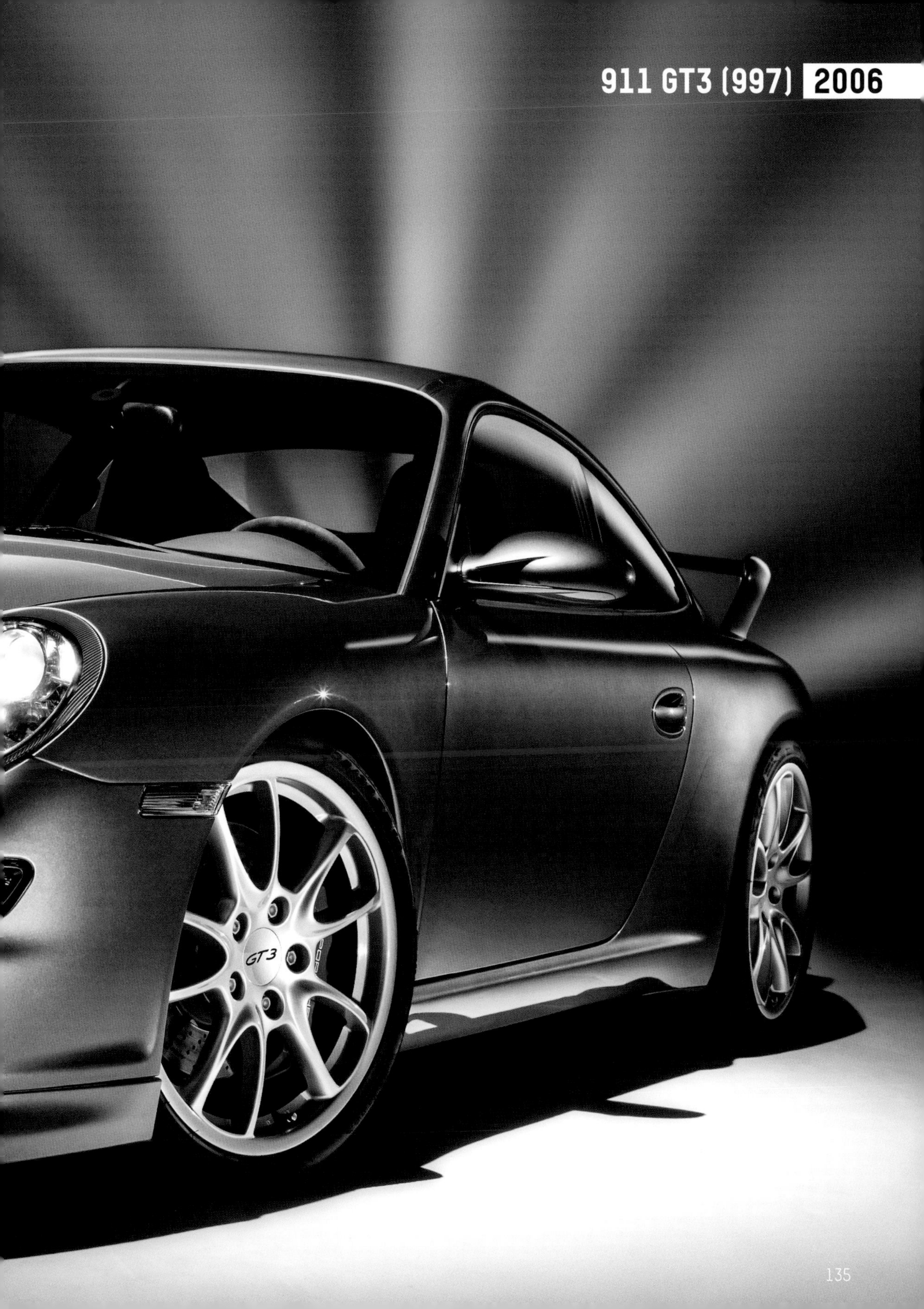
GT3

Year of manufacture	2010
Engine capacity	3,800 cc
Power	408 hp / 300 kW
Transmission	six-speed transmission
Weight	1495 kg / 3,300 lbs.
Acceleration	0–100 km/h in 4.6 seconds
Top speed	306 km/h / 190 mph
Quantity produced	2,656 models

Year of manufacture	2010
Engine capacity	3,600 cc
Power	620 hp / 456 kW
Transmission	six-speed transmission
Weight	1370 kg / 3,020 lbs.
Acceleration	0–100 km/h in 3.5 seconds
Top speed	330 km/h / 205 mph
Quantity produced	500 models

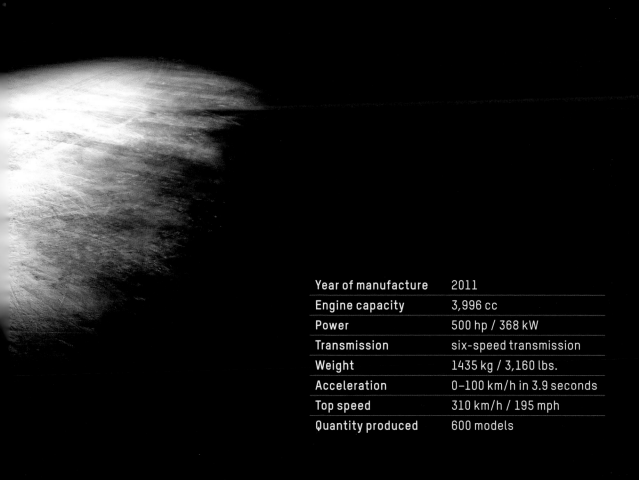

Year of manufacture	2011
Engine capacity	3,996 cc
Power	500 hp / 368 kW
Transmission	six-speed transmission
Weight	1435 kg / 3,160 lbs.
Acceleration	0–100 km/h in 3.9 seconds
Top speed	310 km/h / 195 mph
Quantity produced	600 models

THE FUTURE HAS BEGUN

2011–2018

Of course the seventh 911 generation is also clearly identifiable as an 11. Nevertheless, the newcomer with the code number 991 seemed a great deal different at its world premiere on September 15, 2011, at the IAA in Frankfurt: With its wheelbase extended by 100 millimeters, it offered a roomier interior; the front section had larger air intakes, and the LED lighting strips were new, too. It goes without saying that the engines, at 3.4 liters of capacity for the Carrera and 3.8 liters for the Carrera S, had also been updated and were now more environmentally friendly and—thanks to start/stop technology—more economical than ever before. For the first time, a 7-speed double-clutch transmission (PDK) was available as an option.

DIE ZUKUNFT HAT BEGONNEN

Natürlich ist auch die siebte 911-Generation klar als Elfer zu erkennen. Dennoch gab sich der Neue mit der Codenummer 991 bei der Weltpremiere am 15. September 2011 auf der IAA in Frankfurt stark verändert: Mit dem um 100 Millimeter gewachsenen Radstand bot er mehr Innenraum, die Frontpartie hatte größere Lufteinlässe, und die LED-Lichtbänder waren ebenfalls neu. Selbstverständlich wurden die

Motoren mit 3,4 Liter für den Carrera und 3,8 Liter Hubraum für den Carrera S ebenfalls überarbeitet und waren nun umweltfreundlicher und auch – dank Start-Stop-Technik – sparsamer denn je. Erstmals gab es auf Kundenwunsch auch ein 7-Gang-Doppelkupplungsgetriebe (PDK).

L'AVENIR A DÉJÀ COMMENCÉ

Naturellement, la septième génération de 911 est clairement identifiable comme telle. Cependant, la petite nouvelle, nom de code 991, se montre fortement modifiée lors de sa première mondiale au salon IAA de Francfort le 15 septembre 2011 : avec un empattement élargi de 100 millimètres, elle offre davantage d'espace dans l'habitacle, la partie frontale affiche des prises d'air plus grandes, et les bandeaux lumineux à LED sont également une nouveauté. Bien entendu, les motorisations ont elles aussi été modifiées, avec un 3,4 litres de cylindrée pour la Carrera et un 3,8 litres de cylindrée pour la Carrera S, et offrent une meilleure protection de l'environnement car la plus faible consommation jamais enregistrée grâce à la technique start stop. Pour la première fois aussi, une boîte de vitesses à double embrayage 7 vitesses (PDK) est disponible en option.

Year of manufacture	2011
Engine capacity	3,800 cc
Power	400 hp / 294 kW
Transmission	seven-speed transmission / seven-speed PDK
Weight	1505 kg / 3,320 lbs.
Acceleration	0–100 km/h in 4.5 seconds
Top speed	304 km/h / 190 mph

Year of manufacture	2011
Engine capacity	3,800 cc
Power	400 hp / 294 kW
Transmission	seven-speed transmission / seven-speed PDK
Weight	1505 kg / 3,320 lbs.
Acceleration	0–100 km/h in 4.5 seconds
Top speed	304 km/h / 190 mph

911 Carrera 4S (991)

Year of manufacture	2012
Engine capacity	3,800 cc
Power	400 hp / 294 kW
Transmission	seven-speed transmission / seven-speed PDK
Weight	1520 kg / 3,350 lbs.
Acceleration	0–100 km/h in 4.5 seconds
Top speed	299 km/h / 185 mph

911 Carrera 4 (991)

Year of manufacture	2012
Engine capacity	3,436 cc
Power	350 hp / 257 kW
Transmission	seven-speed transmission / seven-speed PDK
Weight	1470 kg / 3,240 lbs.
Acceleration	0–100 km/h in 4.9 seconds
Top speed	285 km/h / 175 mph

Year of manufacture	2014
Engine capacity	3,436 cc
Power	350 hp / 257 kW
Transmission	seven-speed transmission / seven-speed PDK
Weight	1540 kg / 3,400 lbs.
Acceleration	0–100 km/h in 5.2 seconds
Top speed	282 km/h / 175 mph

Year of manufacture	2015
Engine capacity	3,800 cc
Power	520 hp / 383 kW
Transmission	seven-speed double-clutch transmission
Weight	1595 kg / 3,520 lbs.
Acceleration	0–100 km/h in 3.4 seconds
Top speed	315 km/h / 195 mph

The variety of models increased—naturally, Porsche perfected the eleven range over the next several years. To begin with, in 2013, emphatically sport-oriented buyers were presented with the 911 GT3, lining up at 475 hp—and in 2015, the version designed more with a racetrack in mind, the 911 GT3 RS, was even fitted with a 500-hp, 4-litre engine. Late 2014 saw the arrival of the GTS, a 430-hp model meant to fill the gap between the Carrera S and the GT3. The new 911 Turbo presented in 2015 initially offered 520 hp with 3.8 litres of engine capacity; later on, the Turbo S was launched, delivering 560 hp of power—and joined in early 2016 by a 580-hp version. This was followed in 2017 by the Turbo S Exclusive Series, a model limited to a production run of just 500 specimens. And since Porsche can never offer enough power, June 2017 saw the introduction of the GT2 RS with 700 hp and a top speed of 340 km/h. Those unable to acquire one of the 2,500 limited-production models had another opportunity, in 2018, to line up for one of the 2,000 GT3 RS companion models released to the road with 520 hp. Last but not least, in 2018 Porsche introduced the new 911 T: a somewhat lower-priced, entry-level model.

Die Modellvielfalt nimmt zu – natürlich perfektionierte Porsche im Laufe der nächsten Jahre das Elfer-Angebot. Zuerst erhielten die betont sportlich orientierten Käufer 2013 den 911 GT3, der mit 475 PS antrat. Die mehr für die Rennstrecke konzipierte 911 GT3 RS-Version erhielt 2015 sogar 500 PS Leistung, die von einem 4-Liter-Motor bereitgestellt wurden. Ende 2014 kam der GTS, der mit 430 PS die Lücke zwischen Carrera S und GT3 füllen sollte. Der 2015 präsentierte neue 911 Turbo bot zuerst mit 3,8 Liter Hubraum 520 PS, der später gekommene Turbo S lieferte 560 PS Leistung, denen Anfang 2016 dann eine 580 PS-Version zur Seite gestellt wurde. 2017 folgte der auf 500 Exemplare begrenzte Turbo S Exclusive Series. Und da Porsche nie genug Leistung bieten kann, brachte der Juni 2017 den GT2 RS mit 700 PS und 340 km/h Höchstgeschwindigkeit. Wer keines der auf 2500 Exemplare limitierten Modelle ergattert hatte, besaß dann 2018 die Chance, sich für eines der 2000 GT3 RS-Gefährte anzustellen, die mit nunmehr 520 PS auf die Straße losgelassen wurden. Last, but not least, schuf Porsche 2018 mit dem neuen 911 T wieder ein etwas preisgünstigeres Einstiegsmodell.

Avec un catalogue toujours plus étoffé, Porsche a naturellement perfectionné sa gamme de 911 au fil des années. En 2013, les adeptes de la conduite sportive ont d'abord pu acquérir la 911 GT3 avec ses 475 CH. La 911 GT3 version RS, davantage conçue pour le circuit, a même été dotée en 2015 d'une puissance de 500 CH, délivrés par un moteur de 4 litres. La GTS fit son apparition fin 2014, dans l'optique de combler, avec ses 430 CH, l'écart existant entre la Carrera S et la GT3. Avec sa cylindrée de 3,8 litres, la nouvelle 911 Turbo présentée en 2015 fut tout d'abord proposée en version 520 CH, suivie plus tard par la Turbo S avec 560 CH, modèles rejoints début 2016 par une version de 580 CH. La Turbo S Exclusive Series suivit en 2017, dans une édition limitée à 500 exemplaires. Toujours plus avide de performances, Porsche lance en juin 2017 la GT2 RS, d'une puissance de 700 CH et pouvant atteindre une vitesse de 340 km/h ! Ceux qui ne parvinrent pas à se procurer l'un de ces modèles limités à 2500 exemplaires eurent ensuite la chance, en 2018, de pouvoir acquérir l'une des 2000 GT3 RS, désormais lâchées sur route en version 520 CH. Dernier modèle en date, et non des moindres, la nouvelle 911 T sortie en 2018, permet à Porsche de proposer à nouveau un modèle d'entrée de gamme quelque peu plus abordable.

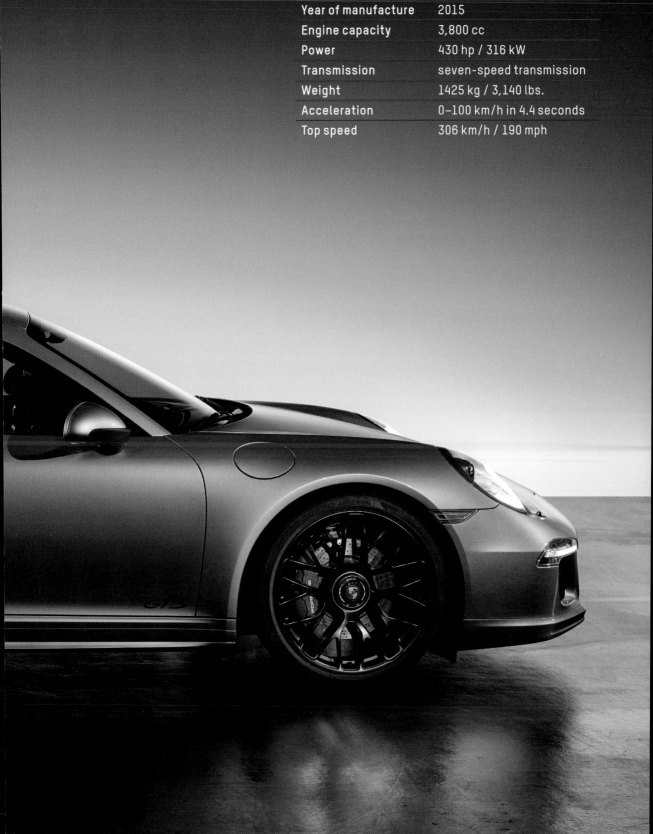

Year of manufacture	2015
Engine capacity	3,800 cc
Power	430 hp / 316 kW
Transmission	seven-speed transmission
Weight	1425 kg / 3,140 lbs.
Acceleration	0–100 km/h in 4.4 seconds
Top speed	306 km/h / 190 mph

Year of manufacture	2015
Engine capacity	3,800 cc
Power	430 hp / 316 kW
Transmission	seven-speed transmission
Weight	1495 kg / 3,330 lbs.
Acceleration	0–100 km/h in 4.6 seconds
Top speed	304 km/h / 190 mph

Year of manufacture	2015
Engine capacity	3,996 cc
Power	500 hp / 368 kW
Transmission	seven-speed double-clutch transmission
Weight	1420 kg / 3,130 lbs.
Acceleration	0–100 km/h in 3.3 seconds
Top speed	310 km/h / 195 mph

Year of manufacture	2016
Engine capacity	3,996 cc
Power	500 hp / 368 kW
Transmission	six-speed transmission
Weight	1370 kg / 3,020 lbs.
Acceleration	0–100 km/h in 3.8 seconds
Top speed	323 km/h / 200 mph

Year of manufacture	2017
Engine capacity	3,800 cc
Power	700 hp / 515 kW
Transmission	seven-speed double-clutch transmission
Weight	1470 kg / 3,240 lbs.
Acceleration	0–100 km/h in 2.8 seconds
Top speed	340 km/h / 210 mph

Year of manufacture	2017
Engine capacity	3,800 cc
Power	607 hp / 446 kW
Transmission	seven-speed PDK
Weight	1600 kg / 3,530 lbs.
Acceleration	0–100 km/h in 2.9 seconds
Top speed	330 km/h / 205 mph

Year of manufacture	2017
Engine capacity	2,981 cc
Power	450 hp / 331 kW
Transmission	seven-speed transmission
Weight	1450 kg / 3,200 lbs.
Acceleration	0–100 km/h in 4.1 seconds
Top speed	312 km/h / 195 mph

THE 8TH GENERATION ARRIVES AFTER 8 YEARS

THE 8TH GENERATION OF THE 911 ARRIVES AFTER EIGHT YEARS

The 911 holds a certain fascination, and it always will. Over the decades, it has become larger and faster—and there are more versions: Coupé, Cabriolet, Targa, Turbo, RS, and many of them with and without four-wheel drive. And yet the essence has remained the same—the 911 is the perfect sports car. The 8th generation, presented on November 27, 2018 in Los Angeles, is a true 911 that is 20 mm longer, 5 mm taller, and it stands more compactly on wider tires. When it comes to propulsion, the 3-liter twin-turbo boxer engine now delivers 385 hp (283 kW) and—in the S version—450 hp (331 kW). The same engines are used in the Cabriolet introduced on January 9, 2019 and in the Targa, which was unveiled for the first time in May 2020. Both also come with or without four-wheel drive. The highlight of the 992 called series is the Turbo, which was introduced in July 2020, always comes equipped with four-wheel drive, and delivers 580 PS (427 kW). Packing even more punch at 650 PS (478 kW), the Turbo S offers amazing driving performance.

NACH ACHT JAHREN FOLGT DIE ACHTE ELFER-GENERATION

Der Elfer ist und bleibt ein Faszinosum. Er ist zwar im Laufe der Jahrzehnte größer, schneller geworden – und es gibt mehr Varianten: Coupé, Cabriolet, Targa, Turbo, RS und etliche davon mit und ohne Allradantrieb. Doch die Essenz ist gleich geblieben – der Elfer ist der perfekte Sportwagen. So ist auch die am 27. November 2018 in Los Angeles präsentierte 8. Generation ein echter Elfer, der 20 mm länger und 5 mm höher geriet – und er steht kompakter auf breiteren Rädern. Für den Vortrieb leistet der 3-Liter-Biturbo-Boxermotor nun 385 PS (283 kW) und – in der S-Variante – 450 PS (331 kW), wobei die Triebwerke auch bei dem am 9. Januar 2019 präsentierten Cabriolet und dem im Mai 2020 erstmals gezeigten Targa zum Einsatz kommen. Gerne auch mit oder ohne Allradantrieb. Den Höhepunkt der 992 genannten Baureihe bildet der im Juli 2020 vorgestellte Turbo, der stets mit Allradantrieb ausgestattet 580 PS (427 kW) leistet – im Turbo S stehen sogar 650 PS (478 kW) für faszinierende Fahrleistungen zur Verfügung.

HUIT ANNÉES PLUS TARD, LA 911 HUITIÈME GÉNÉRATION EST LÀ

La 911 exerce une fascination jamais démentie. Elle a certes été agrandie, est devenue plus rapide au cours des décennies, et les variantes se sont multipliées : coupé, cabriolet, Targa, Turbo, RS, dont bon nombre se déclinent avec ou sans transmission intégrale. Mais l'ADN reste bien le même, la 911 est la voiture de sport parfaite. Aussi la 8ème génération, présentée le 27 novembre 2018 à Los Angeles, reste-t-elle, bien que plus longue de 20 mm, plus haute de 5 mm et plus compacte sur des roues plus larges, une authentique 911. Le moteur boxer 3.0 L de type biturbo développe désormais 385 CH (283 kW) et – pour la variante de modèle S – 450 CH (331 kW), le cabriolet, présenté le 9 janvier 2019, ainsi que la Targa, dévoilée pour la première fois en mai 2020, bénéficient des mêmes motorisations. Avec ou sans trans-mission intégrale, au choix. Le point d'orgue de la série appelée Type 992 est le Turbo, pré-senté en 2020, toujours doté d'une transmis-sion intégrale, qui développe une puissance de 580 CH (427 kW), le Turbo S allant même jusqu'à 650 CH (478 kW) à disposition, pour des performances de conduite fascinantes.

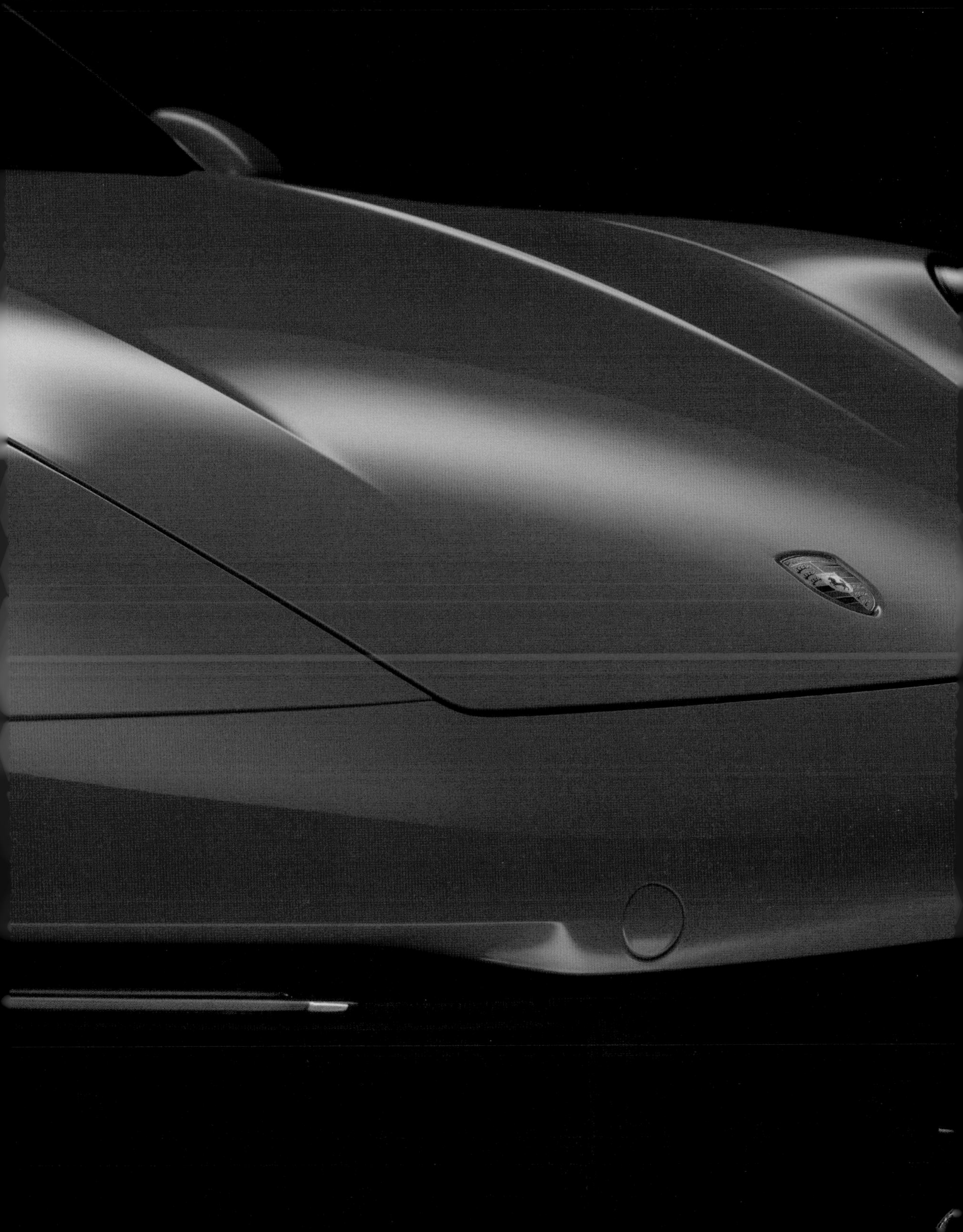

2019 911 CARRERA 4S (992)

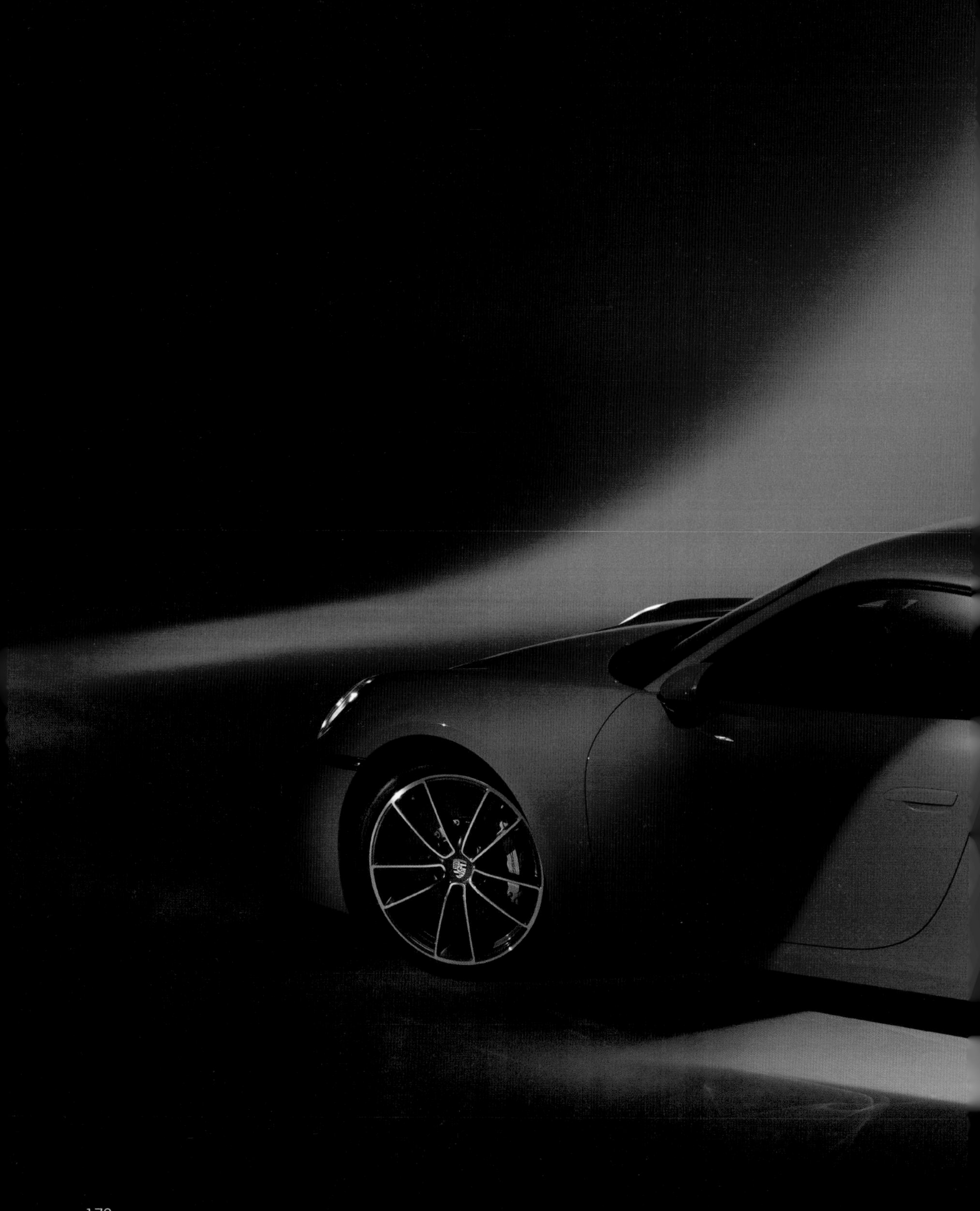

11 CARRERA 4 (992)

ar of manufacture	2019
gine capacity	2,981 cc
wer	385 hp / 283 kW
nsmission	eight-speed double-clutch transmission
eight	1580 kg / 3,480 lbs.
celeration	0–100 km/h in 4.2 seconds
p speed	293 km/h / 180 mph

911 CARRERA 4S (992)

Year of manufacture	2019
Engine capacity	2,981 cc
Power	450 hp / 331 kW
Transmission	eight-speed double-clutch transmission seven-speed transmission
Weight	1590 kg / 3,510 lbs.
Acceleration	0–100 km/h in 3.6 seconds
Top speed	306 km/h / 190 mph

11 CARRERA Cabriolet (992)

Year of manufacture	2019
Engine capacity	2,981 cc
Power	385 hp / 283 kW
Transmission	eight-speed double-clutch transmission
Weight	1650 kg / 3,640 lbs.
Acceleration	0–100 km/h in 4.4 seconds
Top speed	291 km/h / 180 mph

911 CARRERA Cabriolet S (992)

Year of manufacture	2019
Engine capacity	2,981 cc
Power	450 hp / 331 kW
Transmission	eight-speed double-clutch transmission seven-speed transmission
Weight	1660 kg / 3,660 lbs.
Acceleration	0–100 km/h in 3.9 seconds
Top speed	306 km/h / 190 mph

Turbo (992)	
...r of manufacture	2020
...ine capacity	3,745 cc
...er	580 hp / 427 kW
...smission	eight-speed double-clutch transmission
...ght	1715 kg / 3,780 lbs.
...eleration	0–100 km/h in 2.8 seconds
...speed	320 km/h / 200 mph

911 Turbo S (992)	
Year of manufacture	2020
Engine capacity	3,745 cc
Power	650 hp / 478 kW
Transmission	eight-speed double-clutch transmission
Weight	1715 kg / 3,780 lbs.
Acceleration	0–100 km/h in 2.7 seconds
Top speed	330 km/h / 205 mph

WHAT YOUNG MAN DOESN'T DREAM OF A PORSCHE 911...

Developed by René Staud in 1983: the Magic flash® studio lighting system.
Daniel Keyerleber, Uwe Kristandt, Henri Maier, René Staud, Luca Loritz.

...And of course René Staud was one of these young men. But with the aid of photography he found his own way to Porsche, and to many other prestigious car brands, too. "When I was just 12 years old, I knew I wanted to become a photographer, and—after winning four of the five top prizes in a photo competition—at the age of 14 I was able to set up a little darkroom of my own. Logically enough, this was followed by an apprenticeship in photography, and in 1973 I ventured into business for myself with a studio for commercial photography." For a while, Staud photographed everything his broad customer base required, from jewelry to fashions to furniture, until 1983, when he began photographing automobiles in earnest. He quickly sensed that this would be his calling—and today, his studios in Leonberg, Germany, and on the Spanish isle of Majorca are perfectly equipped and well booked.

In an article about René Staud, Christina Ossowski, Head of the Office of Cultural Affairs of the City of Leonberg, defined the basic question for every photo this way: Naturally, photography is in a position to portray and lend an aesthetically pleasing form to any object at all. Whenever it succeeds, though, it is not just objective but, more importantly, subjective: in the choice of the subject, the essentiality of the photographic image, in the choice of detail and in the use of illumination.

René Staud certainly ranks among the leading automobile photographers of the last few decades. As a result, each of his images to commemorate the 50-year history of the legendary 911 bears the mark of its creator, but they go beyond this. They exhibit a remarkable distinctiveness, noblesse and refinement in their placement of color contrasts, of light and shadow, and of compositional weighting in a compelling conclusiveness. Added to this is the photographer's proclivity toward a graduated, deep space in which the levels are imperceptibly joined, and his special sense of texture. Both the studio portraits and the more recent landscapes and architectural spaces with automobiles are amazing for their kaleidoscopic diversity of unexpected perspectives that no other medium can capture the way photography can. René Staud takes the fleeting and lends it lastingness.

Continuing, Christina Ossowski writes: "There are two kinds of photographer: those who find, and those who invent. René Staud ranks among the latter; he stages his photographic work. As with a still life, he goes to great lengths arranging the automobiles in the studio. Thanks to special light sources, light is also incorporated into the staging. Each detail is subordinate to the goal of elaborating the automobiles' distinctiveness, using light, colors and reflections, for a choreography of all of the effects."

WER TRÄUMT ALS JUNGER MANN NICHT VON EINEM PORSCHE 911 ...

... Und natürlich gehörte auch René Staud zu diesen jungen Männern. Doch er fand mit der Hilfe der Fotografie seinen eigenen Weg zu Porsche und zu vielen anderen renommierten Herstellern. „Ich wusste bereits mit 12 Jahren, dass ich Fotograf werden wollte und konnte mir – nachdem ich bei einem Fotowettbewerb gleich vier der fünf ersten Preise gewonnen hatte – bereits mit 14 Jahren mein erstes kleines Fotolabor einrichten. Klar, dass eine Fotolehrzeit folgte, und 1973 wagte ich mit einem Studio für Werbefotografie den Schritt in die Selbstständigkeit." Eine Zeit lang fotografierte Staud von Schmuck über Mode bis zu Möbeln alles, was sein breites Kundenspektrum benötigte, bis er 1983 ernsthaft begann, Automobile ins Bild zu setzen. Dass daraus seine Berufung werden würde, ahnte er rasch – heute sind seine Studios in Leonberg und auf Mallorca perfekt ausgerüstet und gut gebucht.

Christina Ossowski, Leiterin des Kulturamts der Stadt Leonberg hat in einem Beitrag über René Staud die grundlegende Frage zu jedem Foto so definiert: Natürlich kann die Fotografie im Grunde jedes beliebige Objekt abbilden und ästhetisch gestalten. In jedem gelungenen Fall jedoch ist sie nicht nur objektiv, sondern vor allem subjektiv: in der Wahl des Sujets, der Wesenhaftigkeit des fotografischen Bildes, in der Bestimmung des Ausschnitts und in der Lichtigkeit.

Unter den Automobil-Fotografen der letzten Jahrzehnte gehört René Staud gewiss zu den bedeutendsten. So ist auch jedes seiner Bilder zur fünfzigjährigen Geschichte der Legende 911 von seinem Urheber geprägt, sie reichen aber auch darüber hinaus. Sie zeigen Raffinement, Noblesse und eine bemerkenswerte Eigenart mit ihren Setzungen von Farbkontrasten, von Licht und Schatten sowie von kompositorischen Gewichten in selbstverständlicher Schlüssigkeit. Dazu kommen sein spezieller Sinn für Strukturen und seine Neigung zum gestaffelten, tiefen Raum, in dem die Ebenen unmerklich verschränkt sind. Sowohl die Atelieraufnahmen als auch die neueren Landschafts- und Architekturräume mit Automobilen verblüffen durch ihre kaleidoskopische Vielfalt unvermuteter Anblicke, die kein anderes Medium so bannen kann wie die Fotografie. René Staud verleiht dem Augenblicklichen Dauerhaftigkeit.

Und weiter schreibt Christina Ossowski: „Unter den Fotografen finden sich zwei Typen: der Finder und der Erfinder. René Staud zählt zu den Letzteren, er inszeniert seine Fotoarbeiten. Gleich einem Stillleben werden die Automobile aufwändig im Atelier arrangiert. Auch das Licht wird durch besondere Lichtquellen in die Inszenierung einbezogen. Jedes Detail wird dem Ziel untergeordnet, die Eigenart der Automobile mit Licht, Farben und Reflexionen herauszuarbeiten und dabei alle Effekte zu choreografieren."

QUEL JEUNE HOMME N'A JAMAIS RÊVÉ DE POSSÉDER UNE PORSCHE 911...

...Et naturellement, René Staud ne faisait pas exception à la règle. Mais c'est par le biais de la photographie qu'il a trouvé le chemin qui l'a mené à la marque Porsche et à bien d'autres fabricants de renom. « À 12 ans déjà je savais que je voulais devenir photographe et j'ai pu m'installer mon premier petit labo photo dès l'âge de 14 ans grâce à un concours de photographie dans lequel j'ai remporté quatre des cinq premiers prix. Bien entendu, j'ai ensuite suivi une formation de photographe et en 1973, j'ai franchi le pas vers l'indépendance et j'ai monté un studio de photographie publicitaire ». Pendant un certain temps, Staud a photographié tout ce dont sa large clientèle avait besoin, des bijoux aux meubles en passant par les articles de mode, jusqu'à ce qu'il commence sérieusement à mettre en images le monde automobile, en 1983. Il a vite compris que c'était sa vocation, et aujourd'hui, ses studios à Leonberg et à Mallorque sont parfaitement équipés et ne désemplissent pas.

Christina Ossowski, directrice du service de la culture de la ville de Leonberg, a défini ainsi la base de toute photo dans un article consacré à René Staud : naturellement la photographie peut en principe représenter n'importe quel objet et le mettre en scène de façon esthétique. Cependant, une photographie réussie est une photographie dans laquelle tout est plus subjectif qu'objectif : dans le choix du sujet, dans l'essence même de l'image photographique, dans le choix de la partie délimitée, de la luminosité.

Parmi les photographes automobiles de ces dernières décennies, René Staud appartient certainement aux plus importants. Et chacune des photographies qu'il a prises sur les cinquante ans d'histoire de la légendaire 911 est imprégnée du style de son auteur, mais elles vont aussi au delà. Avec leurs choix dans les couleurs, les jeux d'ombre et de lumière ainsi que dans les compositions d'une pertinence naturelle, elles illustrent une personnalité remarquable, la noblesse et le raffinement. Vient s'ajouter à cela le penchant du photographe pour les espaces progressifs et profonds dans lesquels les plans s'entrelacent de façon imperceptible, et son sens particulier des structures. Les prises en atelier comme les espaces paysagés et architecturaux plus nouveaux avec les automobiles étonnent par leur diversité kaléidoscopique de vues insoupçonnées qu'aucun autre médium ne peut capturer comme le fait la photographie. René Staud pérennise l'éphémère.

Christina Ossowski écrit aussi un peu plus loin : « il y a deux sortes de photographes : celui qui trouve et celui qui invente. René Staud fait partie de la deuxième catégorie, il met en scène ses travaux photographiques. Les automobiles sont mises en place en atelier comme un style de vie. La lumière fait elle aussi partie intégrante de la mise en scène par l'utilisation de sources de lumière particulières. Chaque détail sert à atteindre l'objectif final, la mise à nue de l'essence même de l'automobile par l'intermédiaire de la lumière, des couleurs et des reflets et la chorégraphie de l'ensemble des effets ainsi obtenus. »

MANY
THANKS

VIELEN
DANK

MERCI
BEAUCOUP

Harm Lagaay

F.A. Porsche, Ferry Porsche

René Staud, Ralph Lauren

Hans-Gerd Bode, René S...

IMPRINT

© 2023 teNeues Verlag GmbH
Photographs © 2013/2021 René Staud,
Leonberg, Germany. All rights reserved.
www.renestaud.com

sixth printing

Retouching and composing:
  Staud Studios Postproduction Team
Production by Nele Jansen, teNeues Verlag
Color separation by Medien Team-Vreden;
  Robert Kuhlendahl, teNeues Verlag
Texts by Jürgen Lewandowski, www.artandcar.de
Translations by Schmellenkamp Communications
  GmbH; weSwitch Languages GmbH & Co. KG
Copyediting by Esther Caspers;
  Inga Wortmann-Grützmacher, teNeues Verlag
Design by Robert Kuhlendahl, teNeues Verlag
Editorial coordination by Pit Pauen, teNeues Verlag

ISBN 978-3-96171-309-7
Library of Congress Number: 2020936413

Printed in the Czech Republic by
PBtisk a.s.

Published by teNeues Publishing Group

teNeues Verlag GmbH
Ohmstraße 8a
86199 Augsburg, Germany

Düsseldorf Office
Waldenburger Str. 13
41564 Kaarst, Germany
Email: books@teneues.com

Augsburg|Munich Office
Ohmstraße 8a
86199 Augsburg, Germany
Email: books@teneues.com

Berlin Office
Lietzenburger Str. 53
10719 Berlin, Germany
Email: books@teneues.com

Press Department:
presse@teneues.com

teNeues Publishing Company
350 Seventh Avenue, Suite 301, New York,
NY 10001, USA

www.teneues.com

teNeues Publishing Group
Augsburg / München
Berlin
Düsseldorf
London
New York

teNeues